MASTERS OF ART

MICHELANGELO

GABRIELLA DI CAGNO

◆

ILLUSTRATED BY

SIMONE BONI, L.R. GALANTE

MACDONALD YOUNG BOOKS

DoGi

Produced by
Donati Giudici Associati, Florence
Original title:
Michelangelo
Text:
Gabriella di Cagno
Illustrations:
Simone Boni,
L.R. Galante,
Andrea Ricciardi,
Sergio
Picture research and
coordination of co-editions:
Caroline Godard
Graphic design:
Oliviero Ciriaci
Art direction:
Sebastiano Ranchetti
Page design:
Laura Ottina Davis
Editing:
Enza Fontana
English translation:
Simon Knight
Editor, English-language edition:
Ruth Nason
Typesetting:
Ken Alston – A.J.Latham Ltd

© 1996 Donati Giudici Associati s.r.l.
Florence, Italy

English language text © 1996 by
Macdonald Young Books/
Peter Bedrick Books
First published in Great Britain
in 1996 by
Macdonald Young Books
61 Western Road
Hove
East Sussex
BN3 1JD

ISBN 0 7500 1923 9

A catalogue record for this book is
available from the British Library.
Printed in Italy by
Amilcare Pizzi,
Cinisello Balsamo (Milan)

Photolitho:
Venanzoni DTP, Florence

♦ HOW THE INFORMATION IS PRESENTED

Every double-page spread is a chapter in its own right, devoted to an aspect of the life and art of Michelangelo or the major artistic and cultural developments of his time. The text at the top of the left-hand page (1) and the central illustration are *concerned with this main theme. The text in italics (2) gives a chronological account of events in Michelangelo's life. The other material (photographs, reproductions of drawings and other works of art) enlarges on the central theme.*

Some pages focus on major works by Michelangelo. They include the following information: an account of the history of the sculpture or painting (1); a description of the content and imagery of the work (2); *a critical analysis and detailed examination of its formal aspects (3). There are also reproductions of works by other artists, to set Michelangelo's work in its historical context and demonstrate its originality.*

CONTENTS

CONTEMPORARIES

Even in his own day, Michelangelo was recognized by his contemporary Giorgio Vasari as having surpassed all other artists, including the great masters of the past. He excelled as a sculptor, painter and architect and was also gifted as a poet. He was born and grew up in Florence in the late fifteenth century. During his lifetime, in the cultured but often amoral societies of Renaissance Italy, at the papal court in Rome and in the last years of the Florentine Republic, he came into contact with the great figures of his day, from Leonardo da Vinci to Raphael, Lorenzo the Magnificent to Pope Julius II. Yet he remained a solitary figure. He undertook immense tasks single-handed, proudly defending his independence and dignity as an artist.

MICHELANGELO'S ♦ PARENTS
Lodovico Buonarroti and Francesca di Neri. They lived more humbly than their rich and important ancestors.

LORENZO THE ♦ MAGNIFICENT
(1449-1492) Head of the Medici family, art connoisseur and skilled politician, who effectively ruled Florence.

GIORGIO VASARI ♦
(1511-1574) Painter, architect and critic, who idolized Michelangelo.

LEONARDO DA VINCI ♦
(1452-1519) Artist and scientist who was one of the giants of the Italian Renaissance, together with Michelangelo and Raphael.

♦ DOMENICO GHIRLANDAIO
(1449-1494) A painter of high standing in Florence, who employed Michelangelo in his busy workshop.

BERTOLDO ♦ DI GIOVANNI
(c.1420-1491) Medallist and sculptor. Michelangelo went to his sculpture school in Florence.

RAPHAEL ♦
(1483-1520) Painter and architect active in Florence and in Rome, under Julius II, for whom he decorated the Stanza della Segnatura in the Vatican Palace.

DONATO BRAMANTE ♦
(1444-1514) Architect employed by Pope Julius II, and Michelangelo's rival in Rome.

MICHELANGELO ♦
(1475-1564) The greatest artist of the sixteenth century. He was a stubborn character, brusque in manner and solitary by nature.

VITTORIA COLONNA ♦
(1490-1547) A Roman noblewoman famous for her poetry, and a close friend of Michelangelo.

4

♦ **POPE JULIUS II**
(1443-1513)
A great warrior pope, and Michelangelo's most important patron.

♦ **POPE LEO X**
(1475-1521)
Son of Lorenzo the Magnificent, another great patron of artists and writers.

♦ **POPE CLEMENT VII**
(1478-1534)
Nephew of Lorenzo the Magnificent. He directed Michelangelo to create works of art in Florence.

STONE-CUTTERS ♦
Stone-cutters were craftsmen skilled in the use of the metal chisel for working marble, stone and wood. Michelangelo grew up among a family of stone-cutters and, unlike most of his contemporaries, never despised manual work.

♦ **POPE PAUL III**
(1468-1549)
The last pope to employ Michelangelo. He initiated the Catholic Counter-Reformation.

♦ **MARSILIO FICINO**
(1433-1499)
Philosopher and man of letters. Under the auspices of Lorenzo the Magnificent he directed the Neoplatonist academy in Florence.

♦ **ANGELO POLIZIANO**
(1454-1494)
A disciple of Ficino, and one of the major poets of the time.

♦ **COSIMO I**
(1519-1574)
The first Grand Duke of Tuscany. He saw art as an expression of political power.

♦ **ELEANORA OF TOLEDO**
The daughter of the Spanish Viceroy of Naples and wife of Cosimo I. She commissioned many works of art for the Palazzo Vecchio.

♦ **PICO DELLA MIRANDOLA**
(1463-1494)
Philosopher, a leading exponent of Neoplatonism. Pico lived in Florence and was a prominent figure at Lorenzo the Magnificent's court.

SCULPTURE

Florence in the fifteenth century was the centre of a revolution in art. The rediscovery of classical Greek and Roman works of art inspired painters and sculptors to represent the human figure in natural poses and to place their subjects in realistic settings. They made a careful study of human proportions and experimented with new techniques. So, a famous sculpture of *St George* by Donatello appears truly human. His stance is natural and his bearing and facial expression convey courage and determination. In the Middle Ages, sculpture had concentrated on religious themes and was essentially decorative, part of the architecture of Gothic churches. Figures stood out from the walls and were therefore represented from the front only. Now that type of sculpture was replaced by statues in the round: three-dimensional figures intended to be viewed from every possible angle.

♦ ST GEORGE
This figure was carved by Donatello in 1416-20, to occupy one of the niches on the outside of the church of Orsanmichele in Florence. It stands out from its architectural setting (Museo del Bargello, Florence).

STUDY FOR A ♦ DOORWAY
The frame and decoration of this doorway designed by Michelangelo, 1526 (Casa Buonarroti, Florence), show how greatly the artist was influenced by the stone-cutters of Settignano. They were specially skilled in this type of finish.

♦ THE STONE-CUTTERS OF SETTIGNANO
In the Middle Ages, no distinction was made between architect, mason and stone-cutter. The Latin word *artifex*, which can be translated as artist or sculptor, covered them all, in contrast with *operarius*, a simple labourer. Not until the sixteenth century did Italian artists differentiate their work from that done by artisans. In the late fifteenth century, Michelangelo's father strongly opposed his son's interest in sculpture, indignant at the idea that he might become a mere stone-cutter. Michelangelo had become familiar with the tools and techniques of working in stone at Settignano, where he had been put out to a nurse in a family of stone-cutters. Settignano, with its quarries, was the birthplace of Desiderio da Settignano (c.1428-1464) and other well-known sculptors.

♦ CARVING CAPITALS
For generations, the local stone-cutters had specialized in finishing capitals for the tops of columns.

MOULDINGS ♦
A great skill of the stone-cutters was to carve the decorative elements of frames and mouldings so that they would fit together accurately.

♦ **MADONNAS**
In the fifteenth century there was a growing demand from the wealthy Florentine middle classes for small sculptures to furnish their homes. An example is this *Madonna and Child* by Donatello, c.1460 (Louvre, Paris).

♦ **STONE-CUTTING**
Scalpellini, as they were called, were skilled in all aspects of cutting and dressing stone.

♦ **VERROCCHIO**
This *Putto with a Dolphin*, c.1476 (Palazzo Vecchio, Florence), was designed for a fountain. Water sprayed out of the dolphin's mouth and fell back over the cherub. The artist was Andrea di Cione, known as Verrocchio.

♦ **BERTOLDO**
One of the first artists to make small bronzes for collectors was Bertoldo di Giovanni. The influence of classical sculpture is apparent in this mid-fifteenth-century *Apollo* (Museo del Bargello, Florence).

MICHELANGELO'S ♦ **NURSE**
Michelangelo said that he sucked both milk and marble dust at the breast of his nurse, whose father and husband were stone-cutters.

MICHELANGELO'S LIFE

1. *Michelangelo was born at Caprese, near Arezzo in Tuscany, on 6 March 1475. His parents were Lodovico Buonarroti Simoni and Francesca di Neri, a distant relative of Lorenzo the Magnificent. Lodovico's ancestors had held important posts in the government of Florence but the family had lately come down in the world. He was a minor public official and, at the time of Michelangelo's birth, was magistrate (podestà) of the towns of Chiusi and Caprese. A few weeks after the birth, the couple returned to Florence and the baby was put out to a wet nurse at Settignano. Michelangelo grew up during unsettled political times in Florence. At home, he was affected by the negative attitude of his father – an unhappy, discontented individual – and, worse, by the loss of his mother, who died when only twenty-six.* ⟫

DRAWING

Whatever the achievements of Flanders, Venice, Rome and other great cultural centres in the fifteenth and sixteenth centuries, artists in Florence were the finest when it came to draughtsmanship and balanced composition. For the Florentines, drawing was the foundation of all the visual arts – painting, sculpture and architecture. Skill in drawing was the quality that distinguished the masters who ran the workshops of fifteenth-century Florence. One of these was the painter Domenico Ghirlandaio, from whom the young Michelangelo learned the technique of using pen and ink. Drawing was the chosen medium for the preliminary sketch of a new work, for the figure studies and for the final design of the composition as a whole. The growing importance of drawing also confirmed the changing status of the artist in society: no longer a humble artisan, as in the medieval period, but a person of creative talents making full use of his intellectual powers.

♦ A PORTRAIT
Michelangelo drew this *Portrait of Andrea Quaratesi*, 1530-40 (British Museum, London), in charcoal. Generally, charcoal was used for preliminary sketches and studies, because it gave a soft line and was easy to rub out.

PREPARING ♦ THE PAPER
Before drawing, especially with a metal point, the paper was coated with a liquid containing animal bone-dust and the desired pigment.

GHIRLANDAIO ♦
The technique of pen-and-ink drawing was highly developed in Ghirlandaio's workshop. This study of c.1485 was for the fresco painting of *The Marriage of the Virgin* in the church of Santa Maria Novella (Uffizi Gallery, Florence).

PEN DRAWING ♦
From classical times, a common technique was to use a quill pen (from a goose or other bird) and ink (sepia from the ink sac of the cuttlefish, or various other mineral or vegetable substances). The line made by the pen was soft and gave a light-and-dark effect.

♦ VERROCCHIO
The workshop run by Verrocchio, the master of Leonardo da Vinci, was one of the busiest in Florence in the second half of the fifteenth century. This *Female Head* (Louvre, Paris) is a metal point drawing, done on paper primed with an orange-pink ground, a popular medium at the time.

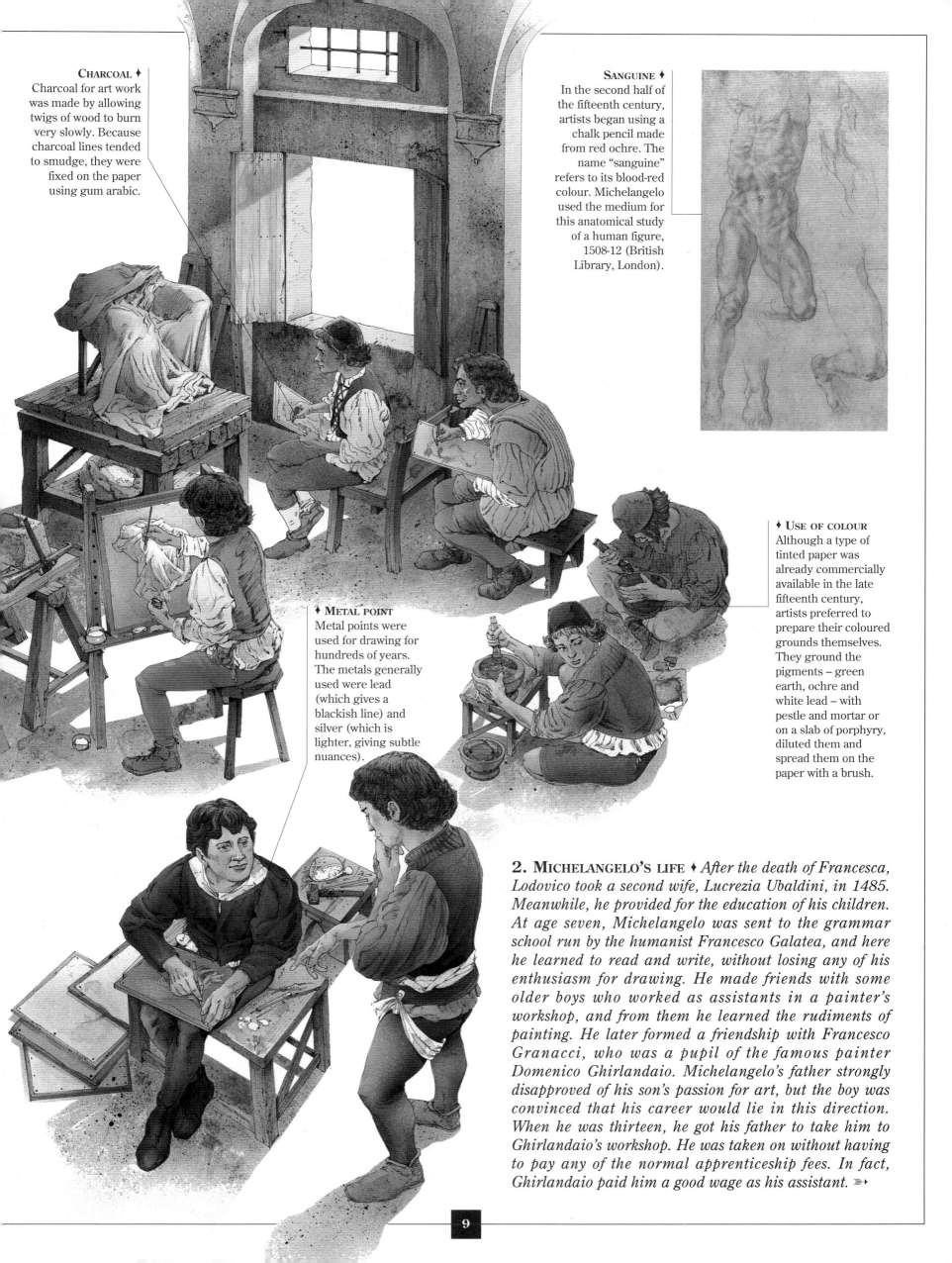

CHARCOAL ✦
Charcoal for art work was made by allowing twigs of wood to burn very slowly. Because charcoal lines tended to smudge, they were fixed on the paper using gum arabic.

SANGUINE ✦
In the second half of the fifteenth century, artists began using a chalk pencil made from red ochre. The name "sanguine" refers to its blood-red colour. Michelangelo used the medium for this anatomical study of a human figure, 1508-12 (British Library, London).

✦ USE OF COLOUR
Although a type of tinted paper was already commercially available in the late fifteenth century, artists preferred to prepare their coloured grounds themselves. They ground the pigments – green earth, ochre and white lead – with pestle and mortar or on a slab of porphyry, diluted them and spread them on the paper with a brush.

✦ METAL POINT
Metal points were used for drawing for hundreds of years. The metals generally used were lead (which gives a blackish line) and silver (which is lighter, giving subtle nuances).

2. MICHELANGELO'S LIFE ✦ *After the death of Francesca, Lodovico took a second wife, Lucrezia Ubaldini, in 1485. Meanwhile, he provided for the education of his children. At age seven, Michelangelo was sent to the grammar school run by the humanist Francesco Galatea, and here he learned to read and write, without losing any of his enthusiasm for drawing. He made friends with some older boys who worked as assistants in a painter's workshop, and from them he learned the rudiments of painting. He later formed a friendship with Francesco Granacci, who was a pupil of the famous painter Domenico Ghirlandaio. Michelangelo's father strongly disapproved of his son's passion for art, but the boy was convinced that his career would lie in this direction. When he was thirteen, he got his father to take him to Ghirlandaio's workshop. He was taken on without having to pay any of the normal apprenticeship fees. In fact, Ghirlandaio paid him a good wage as his assistant. ⫸*

FROM GIOTTO TO MASACCIO

Giotto, who lived in the late thirteenth and early fourteenth centuries, began a movement in Florentine painting which was developed in the first half of the fifteenth century by Tommaso Cassai, known as Masaccio. Adopting a scientific approach to perspective, Masaccio achieved the appearance of reality in his portrayal of scenes, and created solid, convincing figures. Michelangelo was attracted by these great artists from the past and studied and made copies of their works. Florence, under Lorenzo the Magnificent, was now a hive of cultural activity. The medieval view of life was being replaced by humanism. Man was seen as the centre of the universe, free to adopt the role and tasks of his choice and having unlimited potential.

♦ **LEARNING FROM GIOTTO**
The humanists in Florence were interested in the work of fourteenth-century artists, particularly Giotto. Michelangelo's study of two male figures (above left), c.1490 (Louvre, Paris), is a copy of part of Giotto's fresco *The Ascension of St John* (above right), 1315-20 (Santa Croce, Florence). This is Michelangelo's first known drawing and shows how he used the crosshatching technique common in Ghirlandaio's workshop to deepen his understanding of posture and drapery.

♦ **LEARNING FROM MASACCIO**
Far left: Masaccio's fresco *The Tribute Money*, c.1425 (Brancacci Chapel, Florence); and left: Michelangelo's copy of the figure of St Peter, c.1490 (Graphische Sammlungen, Munich). Both give a sense of real three-dimensional space.

THE DELIGHTS ♦ **OF STUDY**
St Jerome in his Study, by Antonello da Messina, 1474 (National Gallery, London). This painting presents an environment typical of the humanist way of life. Jerome is shown in his study, which is furnished with a writing desk and well-stocked bookshelves.

LORENZO ♦ **THE MAGNIFICENT**
An outstanding product of the new humanistic culture was Lorenzo de' Medici, effective ruler of Florence in the late fifteenth century. Patron of philosophers and writers, collector of books and classical works of art, he encouraged the Florentines' growing interest in Greek and Roman culture. He also supported contemporary artists and welcomed them to his various residences. The political stability achieved by Lorenzo created an environment in which art could flourish. Right: a portrait of Lorenzo by Giorgio Vasari, 1488-90 (Uffizi Gallery, Florence).

3. MICHELANGELO'S LIFE ♦ *In Ghirlandaio's workshop, Michelangelo studied painting with great dedication and was soon considered good enough to correct the drawings of his fellow apprentices. His master was quick to recognize his talent. At the time, Ghirlandaio, with the help of his pupils, was decorating the Tornabuoni Chapel in the church of Santa Maria Novella. Michelangelo made many sketches of his companions, so gaining practice in depicting facial expressions and the human figure. At the same time, he took an interest in statuary, going off to study works by Donatello, Ghiberti and other great Florentine sculptors.* ➠♦

♦ **LORENZO WITH ARTISTS**
In this fresco of 1636 by Francesco Furini (Palazzo Pitti, Florence), Lorenzo is surrounded by the artists he patronized. Michelangelo (on the right) is showing his sculpture of the head of a faun, which is said to have alerted Lorenzo to his great gifts.

THE LIFE OF ♦ ST PETER
On the left-hand wall of the chapel, Masaccio painted *Stories from the Life of St Peter*, including the scene of *The Tribute Money*.

♦ THE BRANCACCI CHAPEL
The chapel, in the Florentine church of the Carmine, is named after Felice Brancacci. In 1424 he paid for it to be decorated with frescos.

♦ PARADISE LOST
On the right-hand wall of the Brancacci Chapel, Masaccio painted *The Expulsion of Adam and Eve from the Earthly Paradise*, c.1425. The nude bodies of the two figures (above) are reminiscent of classical and contemporary works of sculpture (for example by Donatello), while their facial expressions are intensely dramatic. These characteristics are later found in figures painted by Michelangelo, particularly in his portrayal of the same scene on the ceiling of the Sistine Chapel in Rome.

♦ ADAM AND EVE
Next to Masaccio's frescos in the Brancacci Chapel there are related scenes painted a year or so earlier by Masolino. *Adam and Eve before their Expulsion* (above), c.1424, is one example. Compared with Masaccio's figures, those by Masolino look much flatter and more static.

IN LORENZO'S GARDEN

A Renaissance garden might be used for growing rare plants, holding entertainments and parties, or as a meeting place for the thinkers and artists who congregated at the courts of princes. Fifteenth-century Florence was the centre of a renewed interest in classical culture, and wealthy people collected Greek and Roman art: sculpture, ceramics, cameos, coins and medals. Most of these were housed in rooms in their palaces, but the larger statues were set up in their gardens. The collection of the Medici family, who effectively held the reins of power in Florence, was kept partly in their residence in the Via Larga and partly in Lorenzo the Magnificent's garden near the Piazza San Marco. Under Bertoldo di Giovanni, this garden became a training ground for sculptors.

♦ MARSILIO FICINO
Marsilio translated Plato from Greek into Latin, and in 1462 founded a Platonic Academy in Florence. This bust of Marsilio was made by Andrea Ferrucci in 1522 (Florence Cathedral).

♦ PLATO AND NEOPLATONISM
The study of Greek and of classical culture led to a renewed interest in the philosopher Plato (427-347 BC). His ideas were compatible with Christian teaching, particularly as regards creation, divine providence and the immortality of the soul. The resulting philosophy, known as Neoplatonism, dominated fifteenth-century Florentine thought. Artists drew inspiration from parables invented by Plato. In his parable of the chariot, for instance, the chariot is a symbol of the human soul, drawn by two horses – passion and reason. The driver is the human mind, whose task is to keep those opposing forces in balance. Above, the parable is depicted in the medallion of a bronze bust attributed to Bertoldo, 1440 (Museo del Bargello, Florence).

♦ PORTRAIT
Workshop of Sandro Botticelli, *Portrait of a Young Woman*, 1483 (Kunstinstitut Gemäldegalerie, Frankfurt). The woman wears a cameo from Lorenzo the Magnificent's collection. The picture on it represents the myth of Apollo and Marsyas.

PLANTS ♦
As well as rare species, some more common plants, such as lemons, were grown in the gardens. Cypress and cedar trees were favourite evergreens.

LORENZO THE ♦ MAGNIFICENT
Lorenzo took great pride in his collection of classical statues. Many famous people visited his garden to see them.

4. MICHELANGELO'S LIFE ♦ *After a busy year in Ghirlandaio's workshop, Michelangelo persuaded his father to let him study sculpture. So he enrolled in the school that Bertoldo di Giovanni, a pupil of Donatello, had set up in Lorenzo de' Medici's garden near the Piazza San Marco. Lorenzo was impressed by Michelangelo's talent and sensitivity and took a benevolent interest in the boy, even inviting him to stay in the magnificent Medici family residence in the Via Larga. From 1489 to 1492, the year Lorenzo died, Michelangelo lived in a cultured, stimulating environment, in close contact with the most celebrated thinkers of the day, Pico della Mirandola, Angelo Poliziano and Marsilio Ficino, who introduced him to humanist literature and ideas.* ➤➤

♦ LORENZO'S CITY
This detail from an illustration in a fifteenth-century book shows Florence at the time of Lorenzo's birth. In the centre is the Via Larga. A little further up are the Baptistery of St John and Florence Cathedral with Brunelleschi's dome. (From *Storia Fiorentina* by Poggio Bracciolini, Vatican Library.)

♦ ARTISTS AT WORK
An arcade had been built in the garden to give shade to the artists working there. As well as Michelangelo, they included Leonardo da Vinci, Francesco Granacci and Andrea Sansovino. The exchange of ideas between them must have been very fruitful.

♦ MICHELANGELO AND THE FAUN
While still a boy, Michelangelo carved the head of a faun, taking his inspiration from a classical work. This particular achievement is said to have made Lorenzo aware of his outstanding ability.

BATTLE OF THE CENTAURS

In Greek mythology, centaurs were creatures with the chest and head of a man and the body of a horse. They were brutish in character and inclined to drunkenness, since they were followers of the god Dionysus (Bacchus in Roman mythology). The myth originated among the mountain folk of Thessaly, a part of Greece that was famous for its horses in ancient times. In humanist thinking, centaurs were symbolic of the wild, animal side of human nature. Michelangelo took his subject for the sculpture shown below from a story told by the Latin poet Ovid in the *Metamorphoses*. This describes a battle between centaurs and Lapiths, a peace-loving people living in Thessaly, who emerged victorious from the struggle.

✦ **A CLASSICAL MODEL**
Ancient cameo with centaur, second century AD (Museo Nazionale, Naples). The myth of the centaurs is the theme of this precious item from Lorenzo the Magnificent's collection.

✦ **THE WORK**
The Battle of the Centaurs, 1492; marble relief, 84.5 x 90.5 cm (33 x 36 in) (Casa Buonarroti, Florence). We know from Michelangelo's biographer, Ascanio Condivi, that this work was finished in 1492, shortly before Lorenzo de' Medici died. It was therefore the last work that the seventeen-year-old artist completed for his patron. Apparently, Michelangelo chose the subject, which symbolizes the victory of human reason (the Lapiths) over brute force (the centaurs), at the suggestion of the humanist Angelo Poliziano. The theme was common on ancient sarcophagi. Michelangelo developed the idea, undoubtedly influenced by Bertoldo, whose school he was attending at the time. The work shows that, even in his youth, he had already progressed beyond his classical models in creating the illusion of space. From the tangle of bodies in the centre the figure of a young man emerges, his bent arm the focal point of the whole composition.
Above and below: two details from *The Battle of the Centaurs*.

Of all the works of his youth, this is the only one in which Michelangelo did not use a bow drill. This was a tool which enabled the sculptor to achieve a perfect finish in every detail. For the Centaurs, *which he later considered to be the best of his early works, he tried something different. Instead of using a linear, geometrical form of perspective, he created an illusion of depth by giving the figures in the foreground a more polished appearance. For the less prominent features in the background, he worked with a claw chisel, which gives a rougher finish.*

✦ **A REPRODUCTION**
Some of the circular reliefs in the courtyard of Lorenzo's palace were reproductions of cameos in his collection. This relief of a centaur was produced in the fifteenth century by the workshop of Michelozzo.

♦ A SCENE BY
BERTOLDO
Battle Scene, bronze
relief, mid-fifteenth
century (Museo del
Bargello, Florence).
For this piece,
Michelangelo's
teacher Bertoldo was
undoubtedly inspired
by a classical work of
sculpture. As on
Roman sarcophagi,
the crowded figures
all appear to be on
one plane.

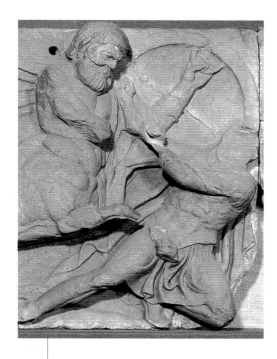

♦ A ROMAN RELIEF
Bertoldo's *Battle
Scene* has much in
common with this
relief on a Roman
sarcophagus, third
century AD (Museo
delle Terme, Rome).
Ancient reliefs were
much studied by
Renaissance artists.

♦ THE BATTLE IN A
PAINTING
*The Battle of Lapiths
and Centaurs* by the
Florentine artist
Piero di Cosimo, late
fifteenth century
(National Gallery,
London).
A typical example of
the Renaissance taste

for mythological
subjects, this
painting is based on
the same story as
Michelangelo's
sculpture.
Piero di Cosimo's
style was highly
detailed and shows
a love of bright
colours.

♦ A GREEK FRIEZE
This detail from a
battle scene is from
the frieze on the
temple of Apollo at
Bassae (British
Museum, London).
Again, the attacker is
the mythical creature
represented as half
man and half horse.

SAVONAROLA

When the Dominican friar Girolamo Savonarola arrived in Florence in 1481, he was well received by Lorenzo de' Medici and the learned Neoplatonists at his court. But, as time went on, his preaching increasingly created a climate of austerity and religious fervour. In 1494, the Medici family were driven out by the people of Florence because of Piero's weakness in dealing with Charles VIII of France, who then occupied the city. Subsequently, Savonarola played a part in introducing a republican form of government, under the sway of his puritanical ideas. However, his austere policies and excommunication by the pope caused him to lose popularity and, in 1498, he was burned at the stake. During his years in Florence, he lived at the monastery of San Marco.

✦ SAVONAROLA
Girolamo Savonarola (1452-1498) opposed the corruption of the Renaissance church and denounced worldly "vanities". Above: Fra Bartolomeo, *Savonarola*, early sixteenth century (Museo di San Marco, Florence).

✦ CELLS
These were the individual rooms to which the monks retired from the communal life of the monastery to sleep or pray on their own. The walls were decorated with frescos showing scenes from the life of Christ, painted by Fra Angelico (c.1395-1455) as an aid to meditation.

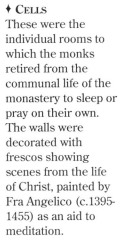

✦ CHARLES VIII
In 1494 the French King Charles VIII and his army crossed into the Italian peninsula, to take the kingdom of Naples. When he reached Florence on his way south, he entered the city triumphantly and effectively occupied it. Below: Francesco Granacci, *Charles VIII entering Florence*, early sixteenth century (Uffizi Gallery, Florence).

CLOISTER ✦
The cloister was a central courtyard, surrounded by a covered colonnade, where the monks would take exercise.

CHAPTER HOUSE ✦
This room was used for meetings to discuss religious matters and, most often, the domestic arrangements of the monastery.

♦ **THE CHURCH**
A door from the cloisters led into the church.

PIER CAPPONI ♦
Charles VIII of France threatened to sack Florence, claiming that the city owed him a sum of money. Pier Capponi, the Florentine representative, tore up the disputed document, successfully defying Charles. The episode is recorded in this fresco by Bernardino Poccetti, 1583-86 (Palazzo Capponi, Florence).

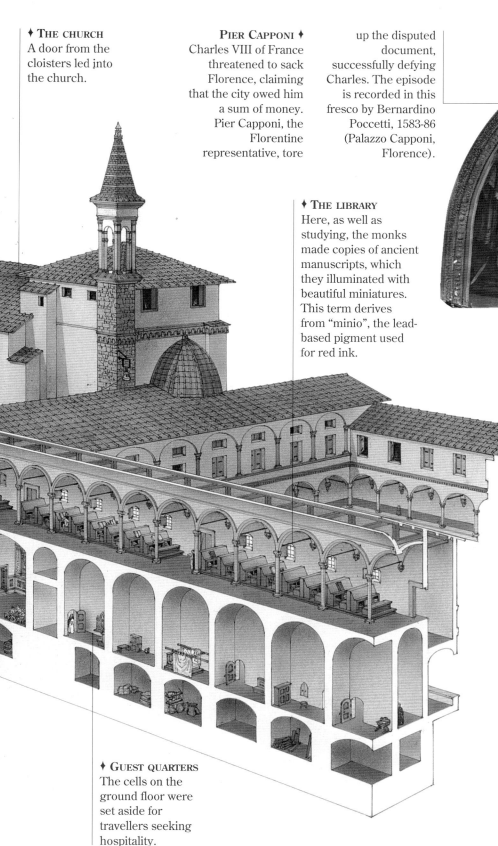

♦ **THE LIBRARY**
Here, as well as studying, the monks made copies of ancient manuscripts, which they illuminated with beautiful miniatures. This term derives from "minio", the lead-based pigment used for red ink.

♦ **AT THE STAKE**
Surrounded by enemies, the Florentines lost faith in Savonarola's ideas. He was accused of heresy, tortured until he confessed, and burned at the stake. Below: *The Burning of Savonarola in the Piazza della Signoria*, 1498 (Museo di San Marco, Florence).

♦ **GUEST QUARTERS**
The cells on the ground floor were set aside for travellers seeking hospitality.

♦ **PIERO II DE' MEDICI**
Piero, the son of Lorenzo the Magnificent, was an arrogant man, lacking the skills needed to govern Florence. When Charles VIII and his army approached the city, Piero fled with all his family. Left: Workshop of Bronzino, *Portrait of Piero II*, 1553 (Uffizi Gallery, Florence).

5. MICHELANGELO'S LIFE ♦ *When Lorenzo de' Medici died in 1492, Michelangelo was obliged to return to his father's house. He did not find this easy: his father and step-mother did not understand him and his brothers were always arguing among themselves. However, he continued to work alone, carving in stone and studying anatomy at the monastery of Santo Spirito, where the prior allowed him to dissect corpses. At this time, he became sensitive to spiritual things and his faith was deepened by attending the church of San Marco, where he heard the preaching of the Dominican friar Girolamo Savonarola. Eventually, unsettled by the threatening political situation and his difficult personal circumstances, Michelangelo left Florence. He stayed for a time in Venice, and then in Bologna. There he became friendly with some of the leading citizens, who introduced him to other artists and even obtained some commissions for him. Having been away for about a year, he returned to Florence in late 1495.* ⟫

ARCHITECTURE

One of the lasting achievements of the Renaissance was to set standards that all later architects have tried to live up to. Fifteenth-century architects, beginning with Filippo Brunelleschi, developed an architectural "language" that was to be used in the West for several hundred years. The great architects of the fifteenth and sixteenth centuries, Brunelleschi and Alberti, Rossellino and Bramante, Leonardo da Vinci and Francesco di Giorgio Martini, never lacked employment. Wealthy merchants asked them to design ever more splendid residences. The rulers of the Italian states wanted villas and gardens. Popes commissioned entire new towns. Constantly in demand, architects tended to become permanent members of the court serving a prince or a pontiff.

♦ **FILIPPO BRUNELLESCHI** (1337-1446) This Florentine architect and sculptor was the true founder of Renaissance architecture, contributing much to the development of the European tradition. His study of surviving classical buildings and knowledge of mathematics enabled him to formulate the laws of perspective. His greatest achievement was the dome of Florence Cathedral, 1420-38 (above).

♦ **LEON BATTISTA ALBERTI** (Genoa, 1404-Rome, 1472) Architect, man of letters and poet, Alberti came to Florence in 1434 and quickly grasped the importance of the ideas introduced by Brunelleschi, Donatello and Masaccio. He wrote theoretical works on painting (*De Re Pictura*, 1435) and architecture (*De Re Aedificatoria*, 1425, in ten books). His own creations include the Tempio Malatestiano in Rimini, Sant'Andrea in Mantua, and the Palazzo Rucellai and the façade of Santa Maria Novella (above), 1456-70, in Florence.

♦ **THE PAZZI CHAPEL** In this early example of Renaissance architecture, 1430, Filippo Brunelleschi combined classical columns, pilasters and arches.

♦ **PALAZZO RUCELLAI** Alberti drew inspiration from classical architecture in designing this residence for the Rucellai family in Florence, 1446-51.

PIENZA ♦ In 1459, Pope Pius II commissioned Rossellino to rebuild the town of Corsignano, near Siena. Working to an ideal plan, between 1459 and 1465 the architect completed the square and the buildings giving on to it: the cathedral and the Palazzo Piccolomini. The town was renamed Pienza in honour of Pope Pius.

6. MICHELANGELO'S LIFE ♦ *On returning to Florence from Bologna, Michelangelo carved a statue of a* Sleeping Cupid. *It was eventually sold through an art dealer to the Roman Cardinal Raffaele Riario, for a much higher price than the sum paid to the sculptor. Riario had thought that he was buying a genuine antique, for the statue had been buried for a while to make it look old. When he found out, he demanded his money back; but he was impressed by the young sculptor's skill and was ready to become his patron in Rome. In June 1496, Michelangelo set out for Rome with a letter of introduction from Lorenzo di Pierfrancesco de' Medici, a collector and patron of artists. In Rome, according to his biographers, he spent hours at a time admiring classical works such as the* Belvedere Torso. *He stayed in the city until the early sixteenth century, completing two of his most famous sculptures: the* Bacchus *and the* Vatican Pietà. ➤

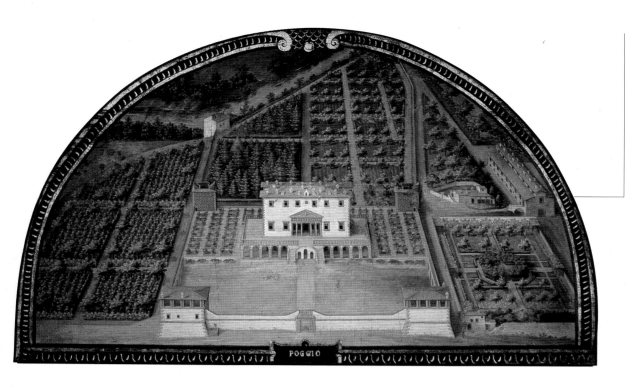

♦ **MEDICI VILLA AT POGGIO A CAIANO**
This painting from the late sixteenth century by Giusto Utens (Museo di Firenze com'era, Florence) shows one of the Medici family's summer residences outside Florence. A fine example of Renaissance architecture, the villa was acquired by Lorenzo the Magnificent and rebuilt in 1480-85, to a design by Giuliano da Sangallo. It was later enlarged by Giovanni de' Medici, the future Pope Leo X.

♦ **BERNARDO ROSSELLINO**
(Settignano, 1409-Florence, 1464) A pupil of Alberti, Rossellino was active as an architect in Rome and Pienza. As a sculptor, he was responsible for one of the most self-consciously classical of all Renaissance works, the tomb of Leonardo Bruni, 1446-50, in the church of Santa Croce, Florence (detail above).

♦ **NICCOLÒ TRIBOLO**
In the first half of the sixteenth century, Tribolo, a sculptor in the service of the Medici, created this statue (Museo del Bargello, Florence) for a fountain in the gardens of their villa at Castello. The influence of Greek and Roman architecture is apparent in the design of Renaissance gardens and in the statues that were made for them.

♦ **DONATO BRAMANTE**
(Monte Asdruvaldo, Fermignano, 1444-Rome, 1514) Bramante had a thorough knowledge of Alberti's classical precepts and was skilled in the use of perspective. From about 1480, he worked for Lodovico il Moro in Milan, where he was a close collaborator of Leonardo da Vinci. He moved to Rome under Pope Julius II and was the precursor of the great period of sixteenth-century Roman architecture. Above: plan for the circular Tempietto in the church of San Pietro in Montorio, Rome, 1503. The symmetrical design, as for a classical temple, is typical of much Renaissance church architecture.

♦ **PALAZZO PICCOLOMINI**
The style and decoration of the Palazzo Piccolomini and the cathedral at Pienza show the influence of Alberti's teachings.

BACCHUS

The Roman god Bacchus (Dionysus in Greek mythology) was the son of Jupiter (Zeus) by the Theban princess Semele. He was traditionally represented with bunches of grapes, his staff wreathed with vine leaves and ivy and tipped with a pine-cone. These fertility symbols referred to his supposed power to grant abundant harvests. His most faithful worshippers were the Bacchantes, and only these women were permitted to celebrate the festivals, called Bacchanalia, that were held in his honour. Other followers of the god included the satyrs, creatures half human and half animal, who were also permanently tipsy. The story of Bacchus is told in Ovid's *Metamorphoses*. This was one of the most popular classical texts among the humanists of the sixteenth century.

♦ **ARTISTS' MANUALS**
To find out how to portray classical subjects, artists would often refer to special manuals. In *Le Imagini degli Dèi Antichi (Images of the Classical Gods)*, 1556, Vincenzo Cartari suggested a way of representing Bacchus (above), similar to Michelangelo's.

♦ **THE WORK**
Bacchus, 1496-97; marble, 184 cm (72 in) high and 203 cm (80 in) including the base (Museo del Bargello, Florence). In late June 1496, when still only twenty-one, Michelangelo made his first journey to Rome, where he was received by Cardinal Raffaele Sansoni Riario, a great connoisseur of antiquities. On 4 July, he began working on the *Bacchus* and finished it in exactly a year. The statue was to have taken its place in the courtyard of the papal chancellery but, in the end, the cardinal refused the work and it was sold to the banker Jacopo Galli, who set it up in his garden. In 1570-71 the *Bacchus* was acquired by the Medici for 240 ducats (Michelangelo had been paid 50). Later, it was placed in the Uffizi Gallery, alongside other classical statues and Bronzino's portrait of *Eleanora of Toledo*. In 1871, the work was transferred to the newly-opened Museo del Bargello in Florence, which houses an unrivalled collection of Renaissance sculpture. There, among contemporary and modern works, its classical inspiration is all the more striking.

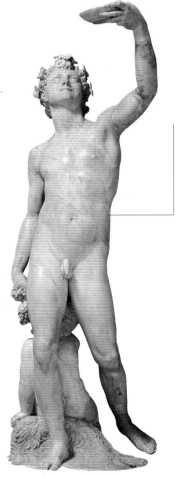

♦ **SANSOVINO**
In c.1514, the Florentine sculptor Jacopo Sansovino carved a statue of *Bacchus and a Satyr*, commissioned by a wealthy patron for his own garden. It eventually found its way into the Medici collection and is now on display at the Museo del Bargello in Florence, next to Michelangelo's version of the same subject.

Michelangelo had already discovered classical sculpture at the court of Lorenzo the Magnificent, but in Rome he was able to deepen his knowledge by studying the Greek and Roman works collected by his patrons. The influence of ancient Greek sculpture is evident in his Bacchus, whose natural pose and careless attitude suggest the god's drunkenness. The little goat-legged satyr, surreptitiously nibbling grapes, acts as a buttress to support the large figure. The highly-finished statue was intended to be viewed from every angle. The garden in which it was originally located would have been an ideal setting.

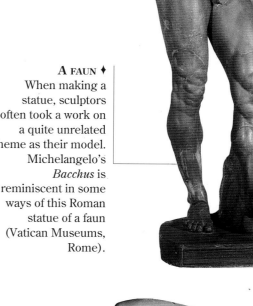

♦ AT THE UFFIZI
In a catalogue of the Uffizi Gallery, c.1750, illustrated by De Greyss, Michelangelo's *Bacchus* is shown to one side of a door in the eastern corridor, in front of the *Portrait of Eleanora of Toledo* and next to a number of antique busts (Uffizi Gallery, Florence).

A FAUN ♦
When making a statue, sculptors often took a work on a quite unrelated theme as their model. Michelangelo's *Bacchus* is reminiscent in some ways of this Roman statue of a faun (Vatican Museums, Rome).

♦ ANDREA MANTEGNA
Bacchanalia with Wine-Vat, 1470-90 (Uffizi Gallery, Florence). This engraving by Mantegna is roughly contemporary with Michelangelo's statue. It shows the festival of Bacchanalia exactly as described in artists' manuals of the time.

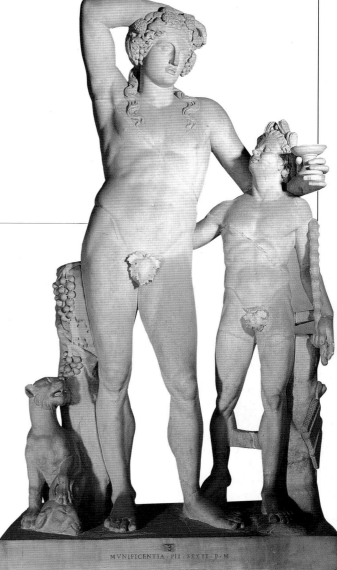

A CLASSICAL ♦
MODEL
There was no lack of classical statues in the private collections of popes and wealthy Roman citizens. Michelangelo may well have been inspired by a work similar to this *Bacchus with Satyr* (Vatican Museums, Rome).

♦ IN ROME
The banker Jacopo Galli set up the *Bacchus* in his garden in the Vicolo dei Leutari. This drawing by Martin van Heemskerck, 1533 (Kupferstichkabinett, Berlin), shows the statue with its right hand broken off, among antique works in Galli's collection.

THE REPUBLIC

In the sixteenth century, the Italian states lost what freedoms they still enjoyed and came under the control of absolute rulers. However, before submitting completely to the Medici, Florence experienced a final period of republican government. After the flight of the Medici in 1494 and the death of Savonarola, the Florentine Republic was threatened from without by hostile Italian and foreign powers, and from within by those still loyal to the former rulers. To guarantee stability, a number of institutional reforms were introduced on the initiative of Niccolò Machiavelli and, in 1502, Pier Soderini was elected *gonfaloniere* (head of state) for life. The new government behaved like any other Renaissance court in commissioning prestigious projects. Michelangelo was commissioned to produce his great statue of *David*, and later he and Leonardo da Vinci were supposed to decorate the Grand Council Chamber.

LEONARDO'S ENVY ✦
Among the crowd in the Piazza della Signoria was Leonardo da Vinci, Michelangelo's arch rival. Neither liked the other, and they had quarrelled. Leonardo was envious of the prestigious commission Michelangelo had received.

DAVID ✦
Michelangelo's statue was so huge that a wall had to be demolished in the cathedral workshops before it could be moved to its new site.

✦ TRANSPORTATION
It took forty workmen four days to manoeuvre the gigantic statue from the cathedral workshops to the Piazza della Signoria.

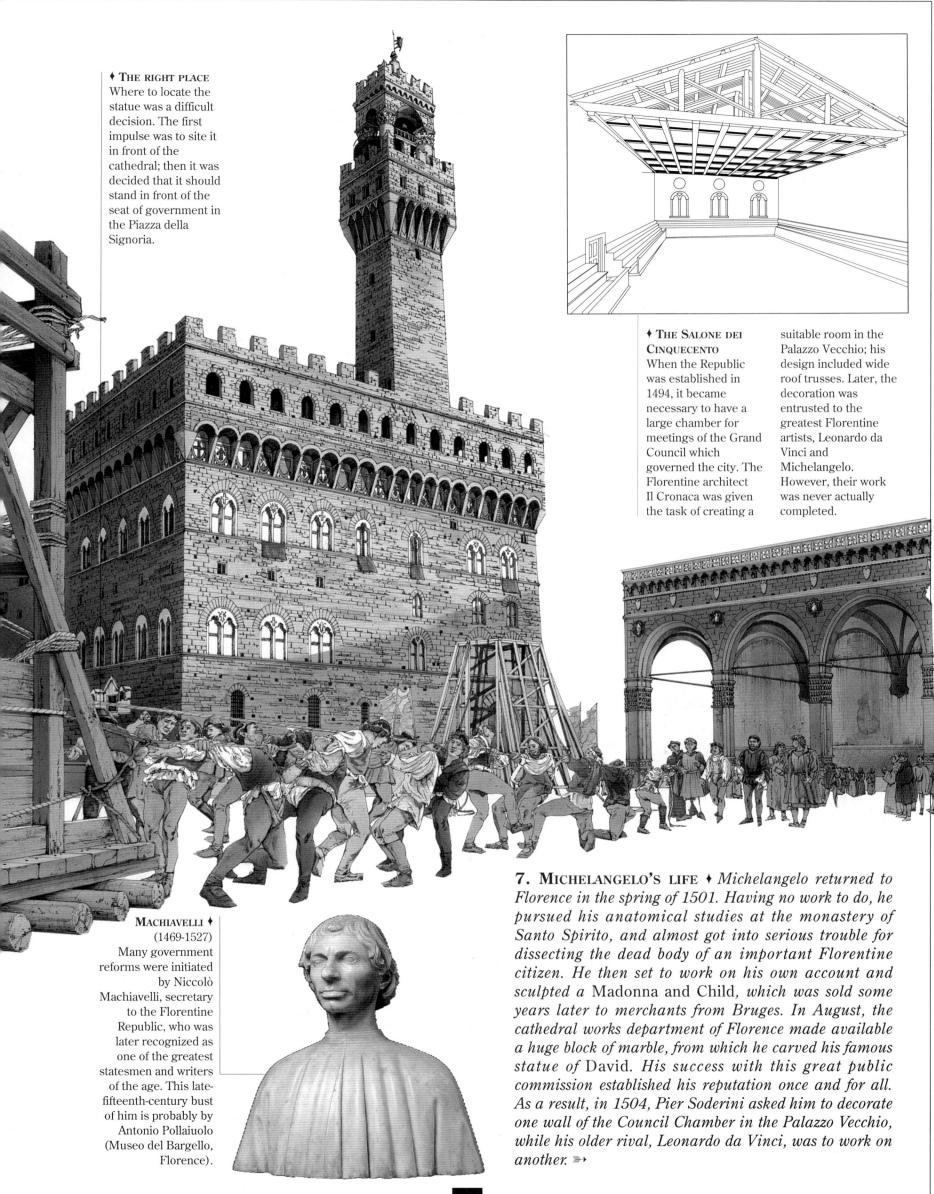

♦ THE RIGHT PLACE
Where to locate the statue was a difficult decision. The first impulse was to site it in front of the cathedral; then it was decided that it should stand in front of the seat of government in the Piazza della Signoria.

♦ THE SALONE DEI CINQUECENTO
When the Republic was established in 1494, it became necessary to have a large chamber for meetings of the Grand Council which governed the city. The Florentine architect Il Cronaca was given the task of creating a suitable room in the Palazzo Vecchio; his design included wide roof trusses. Later, the decoration was entrusted to the greatest Florentine artists, Leonardo da Vinci and Michelangelo. However, their work was never actually completed.

MACHIAVELLI ♦
(1469-1527)
Many government reforms were initiated by Niccolò Machiavelli, secretary to the Florentine Republic, who was later recognized as one of the greatest statesmen and writers of the age. This late-fifteenth-century bust of him is probably by Antonio Pollaiuolo (Museo del Bargello, Florence).

7. MICHELANGELO'S LIFE ♦ *Michelangelo returned to Florence in the spring of 1501. Having no work to do, he pursued his anatomical studies at the monastery of Santo Spirito, and almost got into serious trouble for dissecting the dead body of an important Florentine citizen. He then set to work on his own account and sculpted a* Madonna and Child, *which was sold some years later to merchants from Bruges. In August, the cathedral works department of Florence made available a huge block of marble, from which he carved his famous statue of* David. *His success with this great public commission established his reputation once and for all. As a result, in 1504, Pier Soderini asked him to decorate one wall of the Council Chamber in the Palazzo Vecchio, while his older rival, Leonardo da Vinci, was to work on another.* ⟫→

DAVID

One of the Old Testament stories most frequently
portrayed in Renaissance art was that of David, the
shepherd boy, who won victory single-handed for
Israel over the Philistines. The Bible story tells how
David, armed only with a sling but trusting in the
power of God, took up the challenge of the giant
Goliath, the most terrible of the Philistine
warriors, and defeated him in single combat.
Thus David is also a symbol of liberation
from violence and oppression, and
Michelangelo's statue of him had a
political significance, celebrating
republican freedom as opposed to
tyranny. For this reason, unlike other
contemporary sculptors, Michelangelo
emphasized the heroic aspect of his
subject, depicting David at the tense
moment before the battle, rather than
in relaxed pose afterwards.

♦ HERCULES
This small
Renaissance bronze,
1470-75, once
ascribed to Bertoldo
(Victoria and Albert
Museum, London),
was probably a model
for Michelangelo's
David. The statue is
of Hercules, a
mythical hero
celebrated for his
great strength. The
same pose serves to
express the strength
of David.

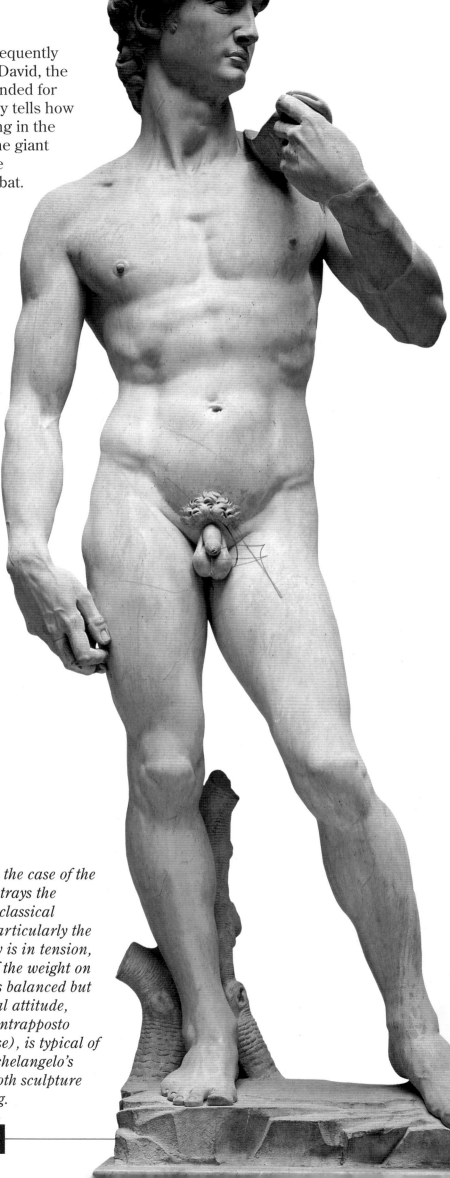

*Michelangelo's
achievement in carving a
colossal statue from a
single block of marble
anticipated what he himself
called sculpture "per via di
levare" (by a process of
removal). This refers to his
practice of gradually
removing material from
the front of the block to
"release" the hidden form
within. The pose of the*
statue, as in the case of the
Bacchus, *betrays the
influence of classical
sculpture, particularly the
way the body is in tension,
with most of the weight on
one leg. This balanced but
asymmetrical attitude,
known as contrapposto
(counterpoise), is typical of
many of Michelangelo's
figures, in both sculpture
and painting.*

♦ **PRELIMINARY STUDY**
A sketch for the arm of *David*, 1501-04 (Louvre, Paris). In the margin Michelangelo noted: "David with his sling and me with my bow", drawing a parallel between the weapon David used and his own bow drill.

♦ **VERROCCHIO**
The most elegant statue of *David* is probably the bronze by Verrocchio, the Florentine artist to whom Leonardo da Vinci was apprenticed. It was commissioned by the Medici before 1476 and displayed in the Palazzo Vecchio. Today the statue is kept at the Museo del Bargello in Florence.

♦ **THE PIAZZA DELLA SIGNORIA**
A detail from Giorgio Vasari's fresco *The Arrival of Pope Leo X in Florence*, 1555-62 (Palazzo Vecchio, Florence). This shows Michelangelo's *David* in its original site on the Piazza della Signoria.

DONATELLO ♦
This bronze *David* by Donatello, c. 1430-33 (Museo del Bargello, Florence), depicts the young hero in reflective mood after his triumph. The figure is modelled according to classical rules of ideal beauty.

THE FINISH

A number of Michelangelo's sculptures are unfinished, and in some cases he may have meant them to stay this way. Certainly, the tendency to leave his works in a rough state became more pronounced as he grew older. Technical considerations apart, there is something deeply significant in this approach to sculpture, which reflects Michelangelo's spiritual outlook. The image that he was striving to release from the raw material represented the perfect but unattainable idea, as conceived of in the philosophy of Plato. At the same time, his struggle to bring forth a pure form symbolizes man's quest for perfection during his limited span of life.

✦ FORM AND MATTER
Michelangelo, *Atlas*, detail, 1513-20 (Galleria dell'Accademia, Florence).

✦ AN UNFINISHED EFFECT
Some of Michelangelo's sculptures are more "finished" than others. In the works of his youth, such as the *Vatican Pietà*, he made extensive use of the bow drill. This tool enabled him to render to perfection the fine details of hair, eyes and other features. The completed carving would then be rubbed with abrasives to achieve a highly polished appearance. Later on, however, Michelangelo abandoned this technique, preferring to leave the surface of the marble "unfinished" and to omit the fine detail. This is apparent in works such as the four *Slaves*, or the *Rondanini Pietà*, a figure that Michelangelo left uncompleted at his death. After 1505, he still used a drill, but for a different purpose and in conjunction with a claw chisel. This technique is also evident in the figures of the *Slaves*. Michelangelo used the worked stone to achieve dynamic or emotive effects, rather than just smoothing out the marble.

✦ MEDICI MADONNA
This *Madonna and Child*, c.1521 (New Sacristy, San Lorenzo, Florence), is another example of a figure left unfinished.

POLISHED PIETÀ ✦
The *Vatican Pietà*, 1498-1500 (St Peter's, Rome), is definitely Michelangelo's most carefully finished work. Every detail is painstakingly rendered, and the surface is highly polished.

✦ RONDANINI PIETÀ
The *Rondanini Pietà*, 1552-64 (Castello Sforzesco, Milan), was left unfinished at the time of Michelangelo's death. It reveals how the artist worked directly on the marble with his chisels, following no predetermined model or drawing, and changing his mind as he went along.

✦ DONATELLO'S LOW RELIEF
In this bas-relief on the base of Donatello's *St George*, 1416-20 (Museo del Bargello, Florence), the background is less sharply defined than the foreground to give a sense of perspective. Here, the sole purpose of the technique is to heighten the optical illusion.

♦ **SLAVES**
These four statues by Michelangelo from 1513-20 (Galleria dell'Accademia, Florence) were originally intended for the tomb of Pope Julius II. They are known as "slaves" or "prisoners" because they communicate a strong sense of being imprisoned in the block of marble. Left: *Bearded Slave*.

♦ **THE YOUNG SLAVE**
Michelangelo first finished the features intended to project most prominently from the block.

♦ **ATLAS**
In the figure of *Atlas*, two faces of the original square block are still evident.

♦ **THE AWAKENING SLAVE**
Michelangelo shaped the marble block with a claw chisel, working his way in layer by layer. The technique is apparent here in the *Awakening Slave*.

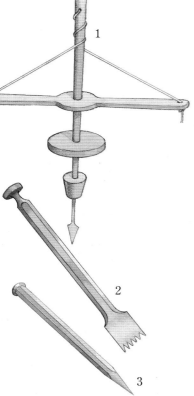

♦ **TOOLS**
Some of the tools that Michelangelo used for his *Slaves* were a bow drill (1) to mark the outlines in the marble, a claw chisel (2) and a punch (3).

8. MICHELANGELO'S LIFE ♦ *The prestigious commission to paint a fresco of the* Battle of Cascina *on one wall of the* Grand Council Chamber *was a challenge for Michelangelo in more ways than one, since his rival Leonardo da Vinci had been invited to paint the* Battle of Anghiari *on the opposite side of the room. Leonardo was an almost legendary figure, and relations between the two men were far from good. The story goes that Michelangelo had even taunted Leonardo for his failure to cast the bronze equestrian monument commissioned by the Duke of Milan. The two artists were very different in both temperament and abilities. Michelangelo preferred sculpture to painting and, of the techniques available, carving in marble to casting bronze or other materials. His sculpture is the expression of a struggle of mind over matter, revealing an inner tension that is the hallmark of his character and life's work.* ➵

CLASSICAL ROME

During the fifteenth century, the discovery of classical statuary, which was unearthed and carefully studied after centuries of indifference, restored Rome's dignity as a cultural centre. From Rome, antique statues, cameos and medals were sent to grace collections all over Europe; to Rome came artists and scholars eager to study the works of antiquity in their original setting. The city was a magnet for artists seeking direct contact with classical culture and hopeful of obtaining lucrative commissions. The great patrons and collectors of the day were the popes, who, in common with princes and wealthy rulers, could enjoy the luxury of private art collections. At the beginning of the sixteenth century, the first open-air sculpture museum was opened in Rome, in a setting created especially for the purpose: the Belvedere courtyard in the Vatican.

♦ A STUDY OF APOLLO
Like most of his contemporaries, Michelangelo was fascinated by the Vatican sculptures. It is clear from this drawing of the *Belvedere Apollo* (Louvre, Paris) that the statue (shown on page 29) had a powerful influence on him.

THE BELVEDERE ♦
It was Julius II's idea to establish a museum of statuary in the Belvedere courtyard. Designed by Bramante in 1505 to connect two separate papal palaces, the courtyard contained gardens and fountains laid out on wide terraces, as well as the museum.

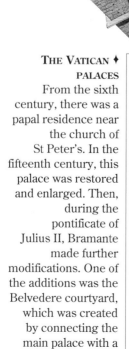

THE VATICAN ♦ PALACES
From the sixth century, there was a papal residence near the church of St Peter's. In the fifteenth century, this palace was restored and enlarged. Then, during the pontificate of Julius II, Bramante made further modifications. One of the additions was the Belvedere courtyard, which was created by connecting the main palace with a smaller residence built by Pope Innocent VIII.

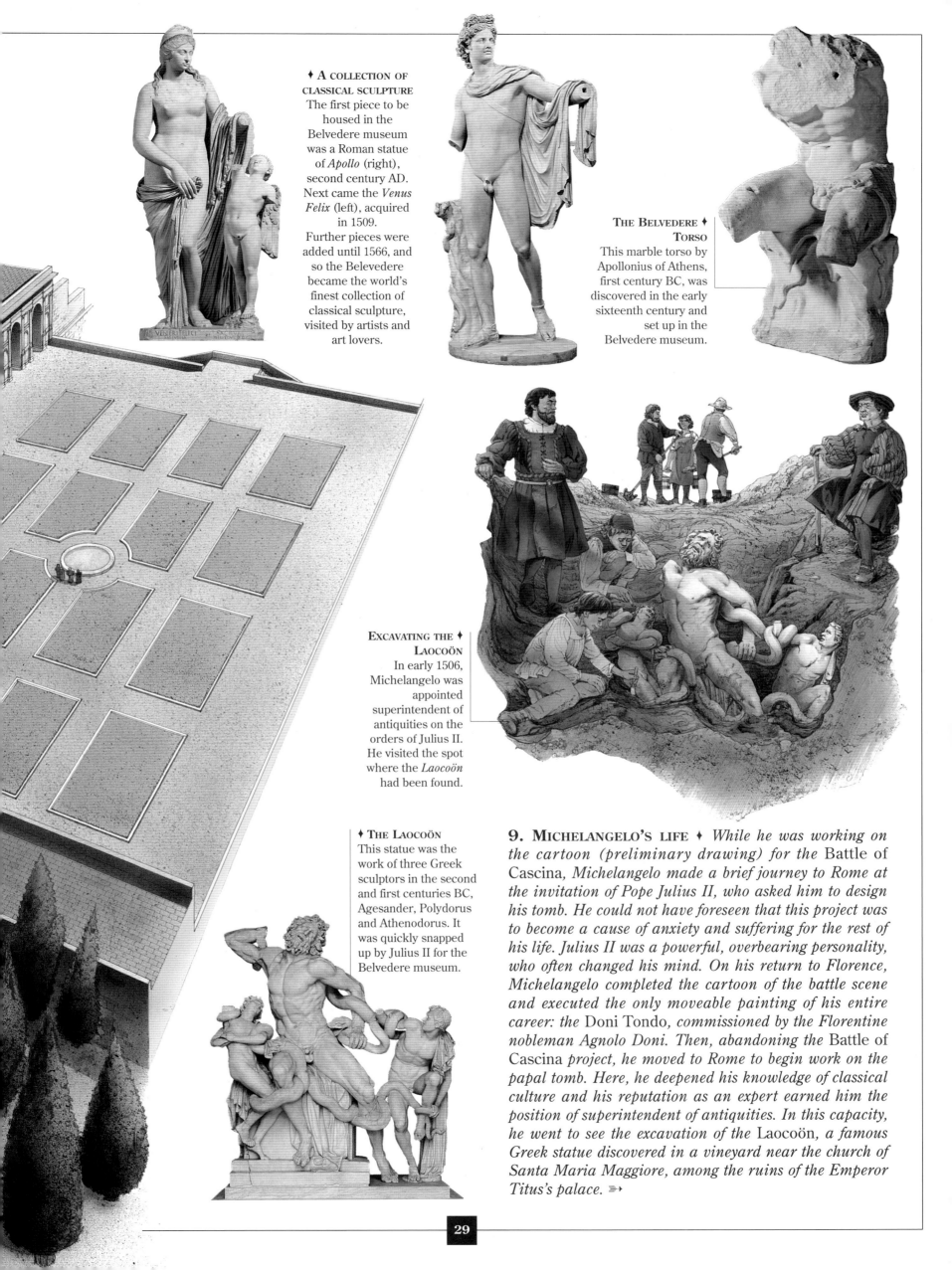

♦ A COLLECTION OF CLASSICAL SCULPTURE
The first piece to be housed in the Belvedere museum was a Roman statue of *Apollo* (right), second century AD. Next came the *Venus Felix* (left), acquired in 1509. Further pieces were added until 1566, and so the Belevedere became the world's finest collection of classical sculpture, visited by artists and art lovers.

THE BELVEDERE ♦ TORSO
This marble torso by Apollonius of Athens, first century BC, was discovered in the early sixteenth century and set up in the Belvedere museum.

EXCAVATING THE ♦ LAOCOÖN
In early 1506, Michelangelo was appointed superintendent of antiquities on the orders of Julius II. He visited the spot where the *Laocoön* had been found.

♦ THE LAOCOÖN
This statue was the work of three Greek sculptors in the second and first centuries BC, Agesander, Polydorus and Athenodorus. It was quickly snapped up by Julius II for the Belvedere museum.

9. MICHELANGELO'S LIFE ♦ *While he was working on the cartoon (preliminary drawing) for the* Battle of Cascina, *Michelangelo made a brief journey to Rome at the invitation of Pope Julius II, who asked him to design his tomb. He could not have foreseen that this project was to become a cause of anxiety and suffering for the rest of his life. Julius II was a powerful, overbearing personality, who often changed his mind. On his return to Florence, Michelangelo completed the cartoon of the battle scene and executed the only moveable painting of his entire career: the* Doni Tondo, *commissioned by the Florentine nobleman Agnolo Doni. Then, abandoning the* Battle of Cascina *project, he moved to Rome to begin work on the papal tomb. Here, he deepened his knowledge of classical culture and his reputation as an expert earned him the position of superintendent of antiquities. In this capacity, he went to see the excavation of the* Laocoön, *a famous Greek statue discovered in a vineyard near the church of Santa Maria Maggiore, among the ruins of the Emperor Titus's palace.* ⟫

THE DONI TONDO

The subject of this painting is the Holy Family: Joseph, Mary and Jesus, with the infant St John behind them on the right. The subject became common in the fifteenth century, especially in Italy, where the figures were usually shown in a domestic setting. In Michelangelo's version, attention is focused on the differences between the generations, and on the relationship with the pagan world. On this side of the parapet, which symbolizes the separation between the Christian era and the pagan world, we find the Holy Family; beyond it is a group of nude figures representing classical antiquity. John the Baptist, also behind the parapet, links the two worlds.

♦ **MADDALENA STROZZI**
A portrait by Raphael, 1506 (Galleria Palatina, Florence).

♦ **THE WORK**
The *Doni Tondo*, c.1506; tempera on panel, 120 cm (47 in) in diameter (Uffizi Gallery, Florence). A commonly held theory is that the painting was commissioned by Agnolo Doni, a member of one of the leading Florentine families, to celebrate his marriage to Maddalena Strozzi in January 1504. The Strozzi coat of arms on the frame appears to prove this view. But an alternative hypothesis is that the work, which betrays the influence of ancient Greek sculpture, was not painted until after the discovery of the *Laocoön* in 1506. In this case, the tondo would not have been executed at the time of the marriage, but to celebrate a birth, which accords better with the subject matter. The Doni's first child, Maria, was born in 1507.

♦ **AGNOLO DONI**
A portrait by Raphael, 1506 (Galleria Palatina, Florence).

♦ **THE FRAME**
The carved and gilded wooden frame bears the arms of the Strozzi family: three crescent moons, linked. The four lion's heads around them were probably an allusion to the lion rampant in the Doni coat of arms.

This is the only finished painting by Michelangelo not done on to a wall or ceiling. A tondo is a circular painting or relief carving, and it may be that this one was to commemorate a birth, its shape perhaps recalling the round table top used in a traditional ceremony to celebrate the safe delivery of a baby. Michelangelo was developing his mastery of contrapposto: the balanced but asymmetrical arrangement of bodies, arms and legs. The sense of flowing movement is similar to that of the David.

♦ **THE LAOCOÖN**
The pose of the nude on the right of Joseph is very similar to that of the main figure in the *Laocoön*.

♦ PALMA VECCHIO
The Holy Family
painted by this
Venetian artist in
1508-12 (Uffizi
Gallery, Florence)
also includes the
infant St John and
Mary Magdalene.
She is identifiable by
the vase of ointment
she is holding, with
which she later
anointed the feet of
Christ. The
composition is more
traditional than
Michelangelo's work.
The colours and
landscape setting are
also typical of
Venetian painting.

♦ AGNOLO BRONZINO
Later in date than the
Doni Tondo,
Bronzino's *Holy
Family Panciatichi*,
1540 (Uffizi Gallery,
Florence), betrays
Michelangelo's
influence, as do the

works of many other
Florentine artists of
the period. The
metallic colours,
elongated forms and
a certain over-
refinement are
characteristic of
Bronzino's paintings.

LUCA SIGNORELLI ♦
A possible forerunner
of Michelangelo's
painting is this tondo
portraying the same
subject by Luca
Signorelli, 1490-91
(Uffizi Gallery,
Florence).

Michelangelo
admired this artist,
whose painted figures
have a sculptural
quality, as do his
own. His is the
work that most
closely resembles
the *Doni Tondo*.

PAPAL ROME

In the early sixteenth century, Julius II, a warrior-pope of exceptional energy, drive and ambition, made Rome the cultural capital of the Western world. Florence and other centres of Renaissance art were eclipsed by the rising star of Rome. The Papal States were one of the key pieces on the Italian political chessboard, and, despite their sacred office, successive popes behaved in exactly the same way as other contemporary rulers: making war, surrounding themselves with philosophers and artists, and commissioning splendid buildings and major works of art. In exercising political power over their subjects and conducting relations with other states, the popes made use of art as propaganda, to glorify their reigns. Among the artists and architects summoned to Rome for this purpose were Bramante, Raphael and Michelangelo.

♦ JULIUS II
(1443-1513)
Nephew of Sixtus IV, and a member of the della Rovere family, one of the most powerful in Italy, Julius was elected pope in 1503. He set about restoring papal power throughout the States of the Church and beautifying the city of Rome. A great warrior, he was overbearing and unpredictable, especially in his dealings with artists. He kept them waiting for hours, and often changed his mind about what he wanted them to do. Above: Raphael, *Portrait of Julius II*, 1512 (Uffizi Gallery, Florence).

♦ LEO X
(1475-1521)
Son of Lorenzo the Magnificent, Leo was made a cardinal at the age of thirteen and became pope on the death of Julius II. As a Medici, he often diverted Michelangelo's energies into projects to glorify his family, such as a new façade for the church of San Lorenzo in Florence. He also commissioned many Roman projects from other artists, including Raphael. Above: Raphael, *Leo X with Cardinals Luigi de' Rossi and Giulio de' Medici*, detail, 1518 (Uffizi Gallery, Florence).

♦ BRAMANTE
Not long after his arrival in Rome, Bramante was ordered to design a building to commemorate the martyrdom of St Peter. Reminiscent of a classical temple, the Tempietto of San Pietro in Montorio, 1503, is emblematic of the High Renaissance.

♦ MICHELANGELO
While Michelangelo was working on the ceiling of the Sistine Chapel, Raphael was decorating the Vatican apartments. In *The School of Athens*, he included this portrait of Michelangelo in the guise of the Greek philosopher Heraclitus.

✦ **THE VATICAN APARTMENTS**
Raphael, *The School of Athens*, 1508-11, fresco in the Stanza della Segnatura, Vatican Palace. Born in Urbino and a pupil of Perugino, Raphael was invited to Rome by Julius II in 1508 to decorate four rooms *(stanze)* in the Vatican. These were used as private apartments by the Pope himself. Raphael completed the Segnatura frescos, on the walls and ceiling, in 1511. Their subject is the relationship between Platonic philosophy and Christianity.

✦ **FONTEBUONI**
This painting by Anastasio Fontebuoni, 1620-21 (Casa Buonarroti, Florence), shows Michelangelo in conversation with Julius II. At such audiences the Pope commissioned new works and received progress reports.

10. MICHELANGELO'S LIFE ✦ *Pope Julius II employed many artists, and this gave rise to a good deal of professional jealousy between them. Michelangelo's main rival was Donato Bramante, the architect commissioned to build the new church of St Peter's in Rome. To spite Michelangelo, who had been commissioned to design a huge, magnificent tomb for the Pope, Bramante even tried to persuade Julius to abandon the project. To add to Michelangelo's troubles, after he had spent at least eight months at Carrara personally choosing the blocks of marble for the monument and had arranged for them to be transported to Rome, they were submerged when the Tiber flooded, and he had to wait for the river water to go down before they could be retrieved. More than once, Michelangelo was frustrated in his dealings with Julius because the Pope, deeply involved in work on the new church, was short of money and refused to advance the necessary funds. In April 1506, the Pope had him turned away by a lackey, and, bitter and disappointed, Michelangelo left for Florence.* ➤

A TOMB FOR JULIUS II

Many great artists seem to have been haunted by one problem that they have struggled for years to solve. Leonardo da Vinci wrestled with the question of how to cast a colossal equestrian statue. Michelangelo's difficulties were caused by his commitment to create a funeral monument for Pope Julius II. The work was commissioned in 1506, and Michelangelo's first task was to go to Carrara to select suitable blocks of marble. The main reason for his troubles was that the plans for the tomb changed many times over the years. He had to contend with a back-breaking programme of work, new commissions, the jealousy of rivals, a lack of funds and, after the death of Julius in 1513, complicated negotiations with the Pope's heirs. Many individual statues, each a masterpiece in its own right, were set aside, until, in 1545, the final, much-reduced monument was erected.

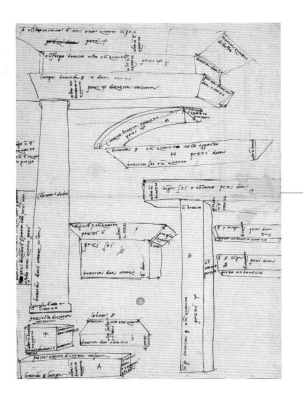

◆ DETAILED INSTRUCTIONS
Michelangelo made detailed drawings to explain the number and size of the blocks of marble that he wanted to have quarried for a particular project. This example from 1521 (Casa Buonarroti, Florence) showed the blocks he needed for the façade of the church of San Lorenzo in Florence. His work on Julius's tomb was interrupted by new commissions of this kind.

MICHELANGELO ◆
Michelangelo journeyed to the famous marble quarries in the Apuan Alps, which dominate the Tuscan town of Carrara. There he carefully selected the marble for Julius's tomb and supervised the quarrying.

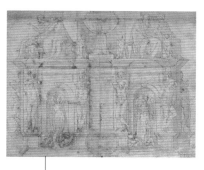

♦ **CHANGING PLANS**
Michelangelo, *Study for the Tomb of Pope Julius II* (Uffizi Gallery, Florence). Michelangelo designed and redesigned the monument many times. His first intention was that it should be free-standing. Then he decided to position it against a wall. He also changed his mind about the number of niches and statues that the monument should have.

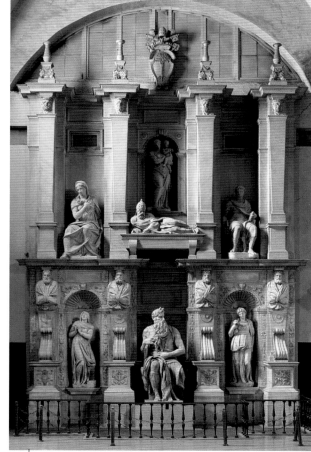

♦ **THE FINISHED MONUMENT**
Michelangelo, *Tomb of Julius II*, 1505-45 (San Pietro in Vincoli, Rome).
The figure of Moses, bottom centre, is the focal point of the composition. This is the only one of the statues that can definitely be attributed to Michelangelo.

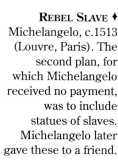

♦ **REBEL SLAVE**
Michelangelo, c.1513 (Louvre, Paris). The second plan, for which Michelangelo received no payment, was to include statues of slaves. Michelangelo later gave these to a friend.

♦ **DYING SLAVE**
According to the second plan, this statue, c.1513 (Louvre, Paris), was to stand in one of the niches of the bottom row, with other slaves or "prisoners" symbolizing the struggle between the spirit and matter. It is clearly inspired by classical sculpture.

♦ **MARBLE**
Marble had been used for sculpture, and particularly for statuary, since ancient times. It was preferred to stone because of its purity, and because it will take a high polish. A very important requirement is that the block of marble should be perfectly sound, as small flaws or cracks in the material will cause it to fracture under the sculptor's chisel.

11. MICHELANGELO'S LIFE ♦ *Despite attempts by Julius II to make him return to Rome, Michelangelo stayed in Florence and started to work again on some of his earlier projects. Eventually, Julius took action to make Michelangelo return to him: he wrote an official letter to the head of the Florentine Republic, Pier Soderini, who persuaded the artist not to cause a diplomatic incident by refusing to do what the Pope requested. In November 1506, Michelangelo therefore went to join Julius in Bologna, which the papal army had just captured. He hoped that Julius would encourage him to continue his work on the tomb, but instead the Pope ordered him to make a huge bronze statue of himself. Then he was directed to take up yet another task. Michelangelo always believed that his enemy, the architect Bramante, suggested this to Julius in the hope that his inexperience as a fresco painter would cause him to fail. The task was to decorate the ceiling of the Sistine Chapel.* ➠

Fresco painting

In Italy the main technique used for painting walls and ceilings was *buon fresco* (true fresco). It was difficult to do, because it involved painting directly on to wet plaster and did not allow the artist to rethink and correct his work. The colours are brushed on and soak into a layer of fresh plaster (the *intonaco*), which dries in the space of twelve hours. For this reason, frescos were painted in daily sections (*giornate*). In the sixteenth century, some artists retouched and corrected their work *a secco*, that is, after it had dried, using tempera (pigments in an emulsion of water and egg-yolk or glue). Unfortunately, these deteriorated quite quickly. In painting the ceiling of the Sistine Chapel, Michelangelo adopted a mixed technique, making some *a secco* additions and changes to large areas of true fresco. The result was a more sculptural effect than had been achieved in fifteenth-century frescos.

♦ THE GROTESQUE
The grotesque style in fresco decoration became popular in the sixteenth century. It included fanciful floral, animal and human shapes, weapons and masks. The name came from ancient Roman buildings called *grotte* where such frescos had been found. Raphael and his assistants used the style for the Stufetta (bathroom) of Cardinal Bibbiena in the Vatican Palace, 1516.

12. MICHELANGELO'S LIFE ♦ *Though he had no liking for bronze casting, Michelangelo was obliged to make the colossal statue of Julius II. He finished it in December 1507. In March 1508 he returned to Florence and bought several houses in the Via Ghibellina for himself and his family. In the meantime, the Pope decided to give him the task of painting the Sistine Chapel ceiling, and in May 1508 the contract was signed. Though apprehensive at so great a responsibility, Michelangelo embraced it enthusiastically and even enlarged on the Pope's original plan. From May 1508 to October 1512, he worked on the ceiling without a break. He built a platform 20 metres (66 feet) high from which to work. He sent to Florence for paints and assistants, but soon decided to tackle the work single-handed.* ⇒➤

♦ MICHELANGELO
We can see how Michelangelo used the *a secco* technique to retouch his fresco work, in this detail showing the figure of the Delphic Sibyl from his decorations on the Sistine Chapel ceiling. Look carefully at the hair of the *putto* in the left background.

♦ GIULIO ROMANO
A pupil of Raphael, Giulio Romano was a brilliant exponent of fresco painting. In the Palazzo del Tè cycle at Mantua, c.1526, he created spectacular mythological scenes, such as this *Aristocratic Banquet* in the Venus and Psyche Room.

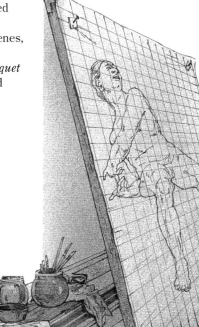

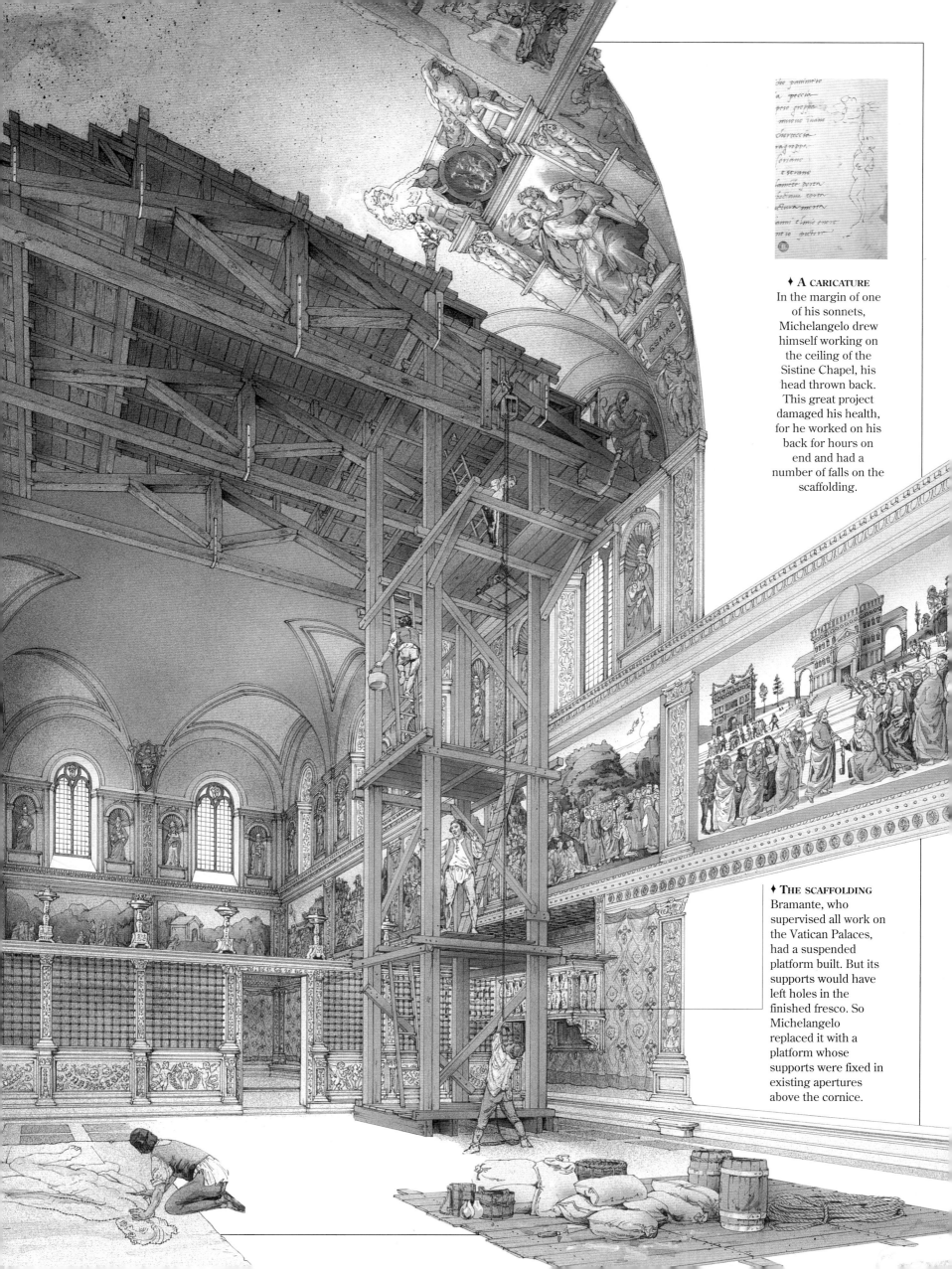

♦ A CARICATURE
In the margin of one of his sonnets, Michelangelo drew himself working on the ceiling of the Sistine Chapel, his head thrown back. This great project damaged his health, for he worked on his back for hours on end and had a number of falls on the scaffolding.

♦ THE SCAFFOLDING
Bramante, who supervised all work on the Vatican Palaces, had a suspended platform built. But its supports would have left holes in the finished fresco. So Michelangelo replaced it with a platform whose supports were fixed in existing apertures above the cornice.

SUBJECTS FOR THE SISTINE CEILING

Michelangelo drew most of his subject matter for the Sistine Chapel ceiling from the Old Testament. In nine rectangular panels in the central part of the vault, he represented episodes from the Book of Genesis, about the creation of the world and the story of the human race until the time of Noah. In the surrounding areas, he painted biblical prophets, sibyls and ancestors of Christ. So the subjects on the ceiling looked forward to the New Testament scenes already represented by other artists on the walls below.

♦ THE WORK
Ceiling of the Sistine Chapel, 1508-12; fresco on masonry, 13 x 36 metres (43 x 118 feet) (Sistine Chapel, Vatican Palace, Rome). The chapel was named after Pope Sixtus IV. The lower parts of the walls had already been decorated by earlier artists and, before Michelangelo set to work, the ceiling was painted to look like a starry sky. Michelangelo received his commission from Pope Julius II, nephew of Sixtus IV, and the initial intention was simply that he should paint the twelve apostles in the spandrels (triangular areas) and a geometrical decoration on the vault itself. But Michelangelo was allowed to put forward his own ideas and the plan became more and more grandiose. With the scaffolding in place, Michelangelo set to work on the painting in July 1508. At first, he was assisted by some colleagues from Florence, including Francesco Granacci, Giuliano Bugiardini and Aristotele da Sangallo, but he soon preferred to work on his own. He completed the work single-handed between August 1508 and 31 October 1512.

♦ DETAIL
One of the bronze medallions that Michelangelo painted on the ceiling.

♦ GOD AS CREATOR
The first five panels, starting above the altar, are devoted to the six days of Creation. In the third, God is shown separating the waters from the dry land and creating birds and fish. These are no longer visible as Michelangelo painted them *a secco*.

Michelangelo began work on the part of the vault nearest to the entrance wall and painted the nine main scenes, taken from the Book of Genesis, in reverse order: the Drunkenness of Noah, the Flood, the Sacrifice of Noah, the Fall, the Creation of Eve, the Creation of Adam, the Separation of the Waters, the Creation of the Heavenly Bodies, and God Separating Light from Darkness.

♦ FIGURES
The frescos on the ceiling cover over 1,000 square metres (almost 11,000 square feet) and include some 300 figures. As well as the nine central rectangular panels, there are eight spandrels with lunettes below them, four corner double spandrels, twelve painted niches and various other spaces which are all filled with figures.

✦ ADAM AND EVE
The area of the ceiling concerned with the history of humankind is above the part of the chapel reserved for the congregation. The painting in the sixth panel represents two related episodes: the Fall and the Expulsion of Adam and Eve from the Garden of Eden.

✦ ANCESTORS OF CHRIST
In the spandrels and lunettes (the triangular and semi-circular areas at the junction between the walls and the vault of the ceiling), Michelangelo painted the ancestors of Christ, as listed in the Gospel according to St Matthew. Above is a detail from the lunette showing Hezekiah, Manasseh and Amon.

✦ THE PROPHET JEREMIAH
Seven prophets from the Bible appear seated in painted niches. Here Jeremiah, who prophesied that the people would be punished for disobeying God, is sitting in sorrowful thought. For his face, Michelangelo may have painted a self-portrait.

✦ THE CREATION OF ADAM
One of the best-known of Michelangelo's Sistine Chapel paintings is that representing God, supported by a group of angels, giving life to Adam.

✦ THE PERSIAN SIBYL
Sibyls were pre-Christian prophetesses associated with particular places such as Delphi and Persia. They are not mentioned in the Bible. However, from the Middle Ages, legends were invented that made it seem that the sibyls had prophesied the coming of Jesus. Michelangelo therefore portrayed the sibyls alongside the biblical prophets.

THE STRUCTURE OF THE SISTINE CEILING

Michelangelo created a unifying structure for the figures on the ceiling by enclosing them in a grid of imaginary (that is, painted) architecture. A rectangular cornice frames the nine main scenes. It appears to be supported by pillars, on each of which sits a male nude. The pillars also serve to create niches, in which the sibyls and prophets are enthroned. At the junction of the ceiling and walls are real architectural features, the spandrels and lunettes; all but the corner spandrels are painted with ancestors of Christ. Thus the painted and real architecture organize the work into three bands – Genesis, prophecy and ancestors.

✦ **ANCESTORS**
The ancestors of Christ are represented in the spandrels and lunettes. They are shown tightly grouped because of the restricted space. This is a detail of the spandrel representing Jesse, David and Solomon.

Michelangelo discarded the rules of perspective used by early Renaissance painters. These were based on a rigidly mathematical conception of space, in which everything was regarded from a single point of view. Instead, his figures are foreshortened in various ways. Their proportions do not respect the normal conventions. The factor that tends to hold all the different figures together in space is sheer energy – the sense of dramatic movement that imbues each one with life.

✦ **SIBYLS AND PROPHETS**
In the painted niches, which look like thrones, five sibyls alternate with seven biblical prophets. All of these twelve figures were believed to have anticipated or foretold some aspect of Christianity. The paintings of them form the band linking the biblical scenes in the central part of the ceiling with the ancestors of Christ represented in the spandrels and lunettes.
Above left: the Libyan Sibyl; and right: the Prophet Jeremiah.

♦ **BRONZE NUDES**
The male nudes arranged in mirror-image pairs in the spaces above the spandrels and below the cornice are painted to resemble bronze statues. Between them is a bucranium or ox skull, a common motif in classical decoration. To paint these purely decorative features, Michelangelo used a cartoon to transfer the design on to the ceiling, simply reversing the figure to obtain its twin.

♦ **PUTTI**
The *putti* act as caryatids, figures supporting capitals in classical sculpture.

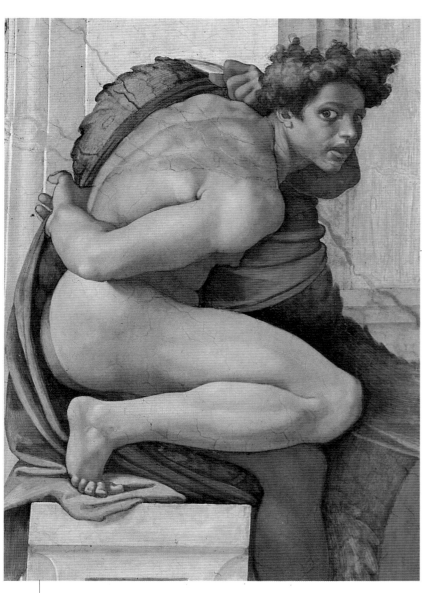

♦ **NUDES**
Above every painted niche is a pair of nude young men. Most of them are holding ribbons or drapery to display a bronze medallion on which a story from the Bible is pictured. These figures fulfil no structural function, but their superbly rendered physiques are reminiscent of classical sculpture. They were probably based on drawings from life, which Michelangelo then idealized and repeated in a number of versions.

HOMAGE TO THE ♦ POPES
Festoons and cornucopias spilling forth oak leaves and acorns are an allusion to the della Rovere family, to which Popes Sixtus IV and his nephew Julius II belonged. (The *rovere* is a species of oak.)

SAN LORENZO

The ancient church of San Lorenzo in Florence was remodelled, starting in the fifteenth century, with funding from some of the wealthy families living in the neighbourhood. The most prominent, the Medici, had built their residence immediately opposite, and San Lorenzo became in effect their family church, enlarged and embellished to enhance their prestige. Filippo Brunelleschi started work on the church in 1419. His design was to make San Lorenzo Florence's first Renaissance church. He was responsible for the main nave and the Old Sacristy. The façade was supposed to have been designed by Michelangelo, but the project foundered. He did, however, design the New Sacristy and the Laurentian Library. Finally, the Princes' Chapel was added in the seventeenth century.

♦THE CUPOLA
The imposing dome crowning the Princes' Chapel was erected in the seventeenth century. A monument to Medici vanity, it dwarfs the domes of the other two chapels.

♦THE PRINCES' CHAPEL
The third Medici mausoleum was built entirely with marble and semi-precious stones *(pietre dure)* in the seventeenth century.

♦ THE OLD SACRISTY
The first chapel intended to house the Medici tombs was built by Filippo Brunelleschi in 1421-28. He adopted a straightforward geometrical style with very simple decoration.

♦THE ENTRANCE TO THE LIBRARY
The stairway in *pietra serena* (a grey stone), designed by Michelangelo and built by Vasari, c.1558, almost fills the entrance area.

THE LIBRARY ♦
The Laurentian Library is not a library of religious books. It was started as a private library by Cosimo il Vecchio, father of Lorenzo the Magnificent, and contains precious fifteenth-century manuscripts.

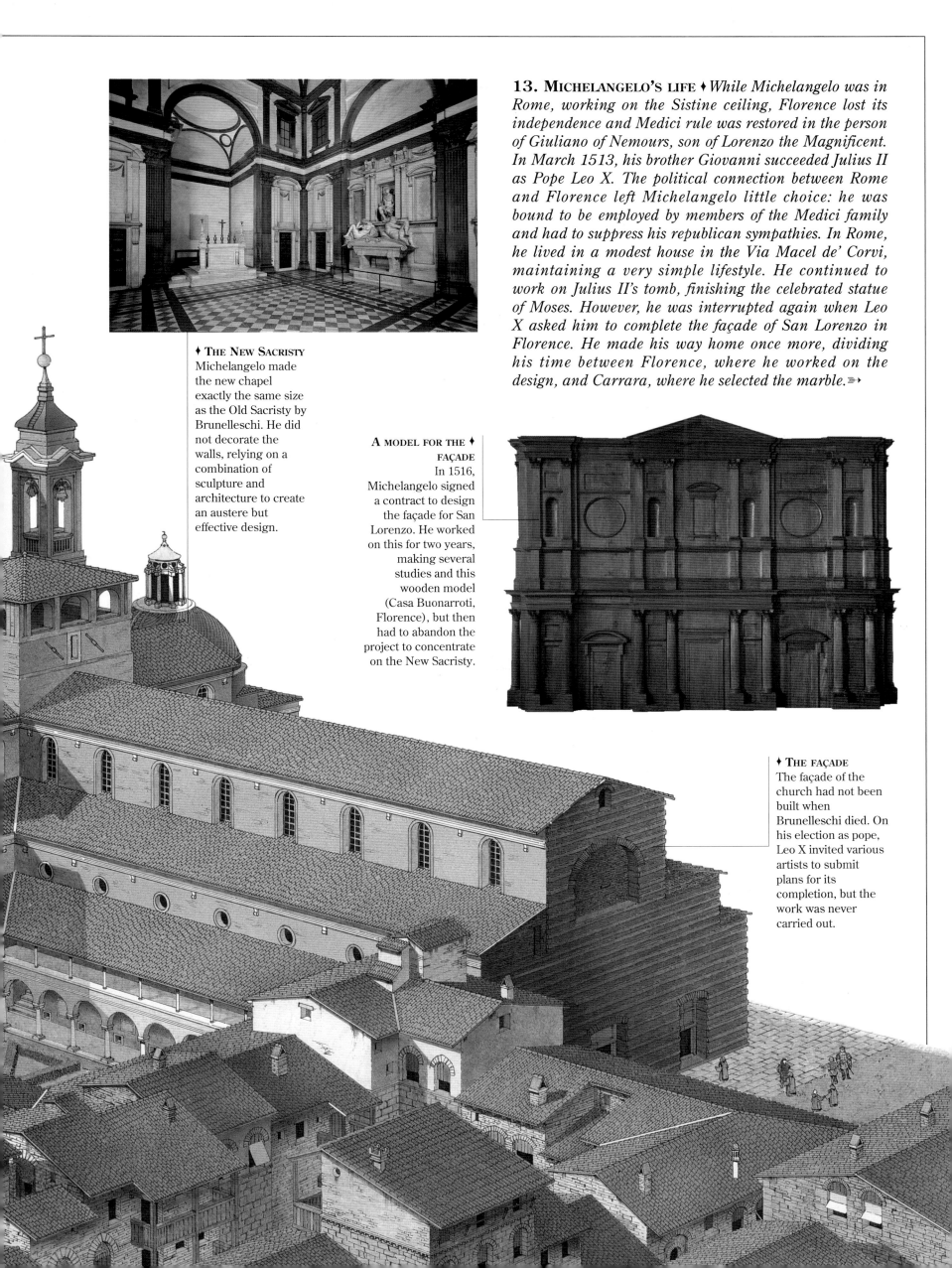

13. MICHELANGELO'S LIFE ♦ *While Michelangelo was in Rome, working on the Sistine ceiling, Florence lost its independence and Medici rule was restored in the person of Giuliano of Nemours, son of Lorenzo the Magnificent. In March 1513, his brother Giovanni succeeded Julius II as Pope Leo X. The political connection between Rome and Florence left Michelangelo little choice: he was bound to be employed by members of the Medici family and had to suppress his republican sympathies. In Rome, he lived in a modest house in the Via Macel de' Corvi, maintaining a very simple lifestyle. He continued to work on Julius II's tomb, finishing the celebrated statue of Moses. However, he was interrupted again when Leo X asked him to complete the façade of San Lorenzo in Florence. He made his way home once more, dividing his time between Florence, where he worked on the design, and Carrara, where he selected the marble.* ➠

♦ **THE NEW SACRISTY**
Michelangelo made the new chapel exactly the same size as the Old Sacristy by Brunelleschi. He did not decorate the walls, relying on a combination of sculpture and architecture to create an austere but effective design.

A MODEL FOR THE ♦ FAÇADE
In 1516, Michelangelo signed a contract to design the façade for San Lorenzo. He worked on this for two years, making several studies and this wooden model (Casa Buonarroti, Florence), but then had to abandon the project to concentrate on the New Sacristy.

♦ **THE FAÇADE**
The façade of the church had not been built when Brunelleschi died. On his election as pope, Leo X invited various artists to submit plans for its completion, but the work was never carried out.

THE MEDICI TOMBS

In his monuments to the Medici dukes, Lorenzo of Urbino and Giuliano of Nemours, Michelangelo tackled the themes of death and life beyond the grave. To express the idea of the dukes' passing from this earthly realm to a higher plane of existence, he adopted a complex set of symbols. At the lowest level of the tombs are the sarcophagi containing the mortal remains of the dukes. On top of these are two pairs of allegorical figures, Day and Night and Dawn and Dusk, representing the passage of time to which everyone on Earth is subject. Above them are statues of the princes, idealized portraits expressing the inner nature of the two men.

♦ **THE WORK**
Tombs of Dukes Lorenzo of Urbino and Giuliano of Nemours, 1524-34; marble (New Sacristy, San Lorenzo, Florence).
A funeral monument for Lorenzo the Magnificent and his brother Giuliano, together with Lorenzo's son and grandson, Giuliano, Duke of Nemours, and Lorenzo, Duke of Urbino, was the idea of Pope Leo X and Cardinal Giulio de' Medici. As things turned out, Michelangelo completed the tombs of only the two younger relatives. He accepted the commission in 1520, and in 1521 went to Carrara to select the marble. However, he did not make much progress until 1524, when Giulio de' Medici was elected pope with the title of Clement VII. No more was done after 1534, when Michelangelo finally left Florence to settle in Rome. He drew up a number of plans for the monument. His first idea was to construct a square tomb in the centre of the chapel, but he eventually decided on a combination of architecture and sculpture, set against the walls.
Above and below: details of the tombs.

♦ **THE TWO DUKES**
The figures of Lorenzo (above) and Giuliano (below) were intended to express the characters of the two men. Lorenzo is shown in a pensive attitude. Giuliano looks confident. His face is reminiscent of Michelangelo's *David*.

In the Old Sacristy of San Lorenzo, by Brunelleschi, the paintings and sculptures serve to decorate the architectural structure. By contrast, in the New Sacristy, Michelangelo achieved a superb blend of sculpture and architecture, *so that the two are combined in one complete work. The figures in the dukes' tombs are framed so harmoniously by columns, niches and blank windows that the work might be described as a piece of architectural sculpture.*

♦ **DAWN AND DUSK**
Left and right: the figures of Dawn and Dusk from the tomb of Lorenzo. The brief period before sunrise and the contrasting moment of twilight, immediately after sunset, are poignant reminders of the fleeting quality of human life.

♦ **DAY AND NIGHT**
Above: The figures of Day and Night from the tomb of Giuliano. Night is the most recognizable of the allegorical figures. Her pose is that of a woman between sleep and waking. She wears a diadem crowned with a star and a crescent moon. The poppies on the cushion beneath her foot are a symbol of sleep. The owl is a creature of the night. The figure of Day is in contrapposto attitude, limbs held in tension.

♦ **RISING FROM THE TOMB**
On both the tombs, the allegorical figures representing opposite moments of the day have their backs to each other. Their weight seems to press down on the lid of the sarcophagus, disrupting its smooth contour. Between the figures is a kind of opening. It is almost as if the figure of the duke, immediately above, has risen through this opening, ascending to a higher level of existence beyond death.

FORTIFICATIONS

In the mid-fifteenth century, the art of war was revolutionized by the introduction of mobile siege artillery which was effective at long range. Medieval fortification systems, with long sections of wall and the occasional tower, became obsolete. For a hundred years or so, the greatest contemporary architects, from Leonardo da Vinci to Francesco di Giorgio Martini and Michelangelo, studied new, more practical defensive structures. In particular, they designed bastions at gates and corners. Defenders on the bastion could catch the enemy in a crossfire, so keeping control of access to the walls and delaying all-out attacks. Having restored its republican form of government in 1527, the city of Florence modernized its defences to withstand hostile powers. In 1529-30, the city was besieged by the troops of Charles V, who two years earlier had sacked Rome.

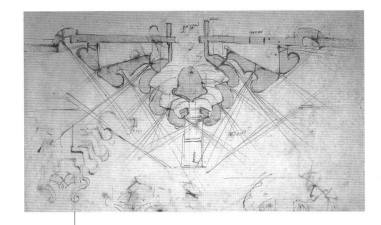

♦ **MICHELANGELO'S DESIGNS**
Michelangelo's many drawings of bastions show an ability to combine artistic shapes with practical considerations. Instead of the traditional square or triangular structures, which were unequal to the challenge of the new offensive strategies, he designed more organic shapes. This drawing of 1528 (Casa Buonarroti, Florence) shows one such structure: the three curved salients are reminiscent of the claws of a crab.

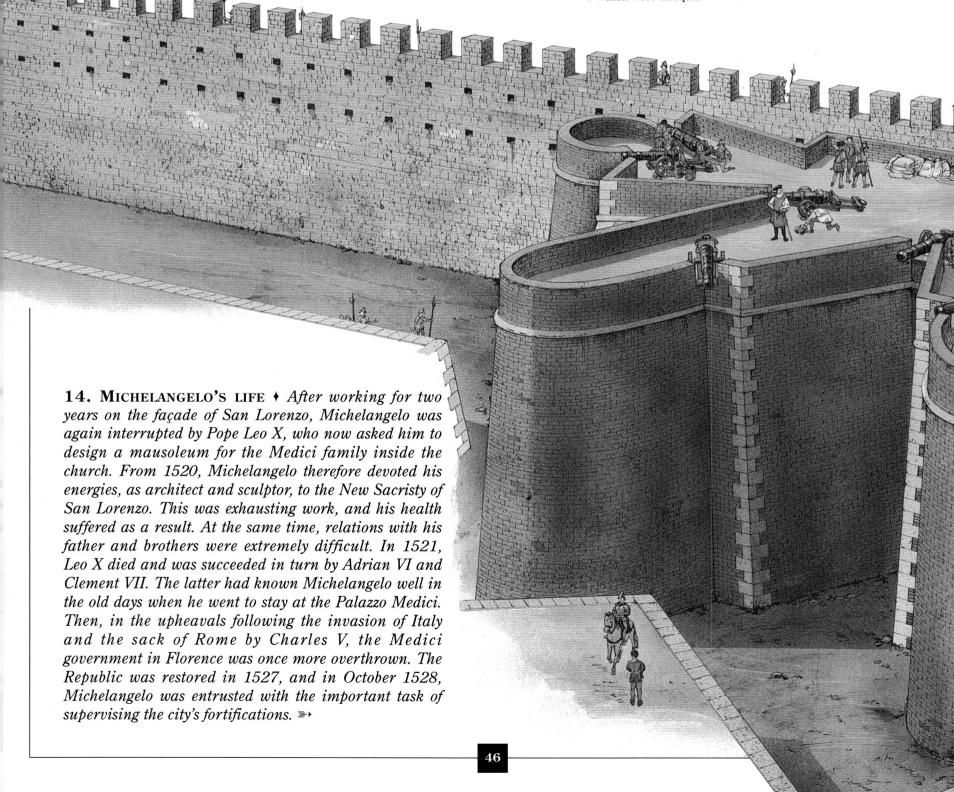

14. MICHELANGELO'S LIFE ♦ *After working for two years on the façade of San Lorenzo, Michelangelo was again interrupted by Pope Leo X, who now asked him to design a mausoleum for the Medici family inside the church. From 1520, Michelangelo therefore devoted his energies, as architect and sculptor, to the New Sacristy of San Lorenzo. This was exhausting work, and his health suffered as a result. At the same time, relations with his father and brothers were extremely difficult. In 1521, Leo X died and was succeeded in turn by Adrian VI and Clement VII. The latter had known Michelangelo well in the old days when he went to stay at the Palazzo Medici. Then, in the upheavals following the invasion of Italy and the sack of Rome by Charles V, the Medici government in Florence was once more overthrown. The Republic was restored in 1527, and in October 1528, Michelangelo was entrusted with the important task of supervising the city's fortifications.* ≫•

THE SIEGE ♦
The siege of Florence lasted ten months, ending in August 1530 when Charles V's troops entered the city and the Medici were returned to power. Vasari painted this fresco of the siege in 1555-62 (Leo X apartment, Palazzo Vecchio, Florence).

♦ BASTIONS
Weapons such as cannon could be installed on top of a bastion, which was a kind of fort thrusting out from an angle of a wall. The crab's claw-shaped bastion, designed by Michelangelo, allowed the defenders to fire in all directions and even to aim at enemy attackers who thought they had reached safety in the shelter of the bastion's walls.

♦ CHARLES V
Titian, *Emperor Charles V on Horseback*, 1548, detail (Prado, Madrid).

♦ MICHELANGELO
Matteo Rosselli, *Michelangelo as Commissioner for Fortifications*, 1615 (Casa Buonarroti, Florence).

GRAND DUKES

♦ **COSIMO I**
This bust by Benvenuto Cellini, 1545 (Museo del Bargello, Florence), portrays Cosimo I as a Roman emperor. Having become Duke in 1537, Cosimo consolidated his position by marrying Eleanora of Toledo, daughter of the powerful Spanish Viceroy in Italy. In 1569, the Pope elevated him to the rank of Grand Duke, higher than any other Italian prince.

Pope Clement VII formed an alliance with Charles V, thus ensuring the defeat of the Florentine Republic in 1530 and the triumphant return of the Medici to Florence. In 1537, Alessandro, the last representative of the senior branch of the family, was murdered. His successor was Cosimo I, who later became the first Grand Duke of Tuscany. Shrewdly combining the waging of war, marriage alliances and diplomacy, Cosimo extended his power over the whole of Tuscany, annexing other cities in the region, including Siena in 1555. Cosimo also promoted the arts as a way of enhancing the prestige of the Florentine state and the Medici dynasty. Many works were commissioned for this purpose during the sixteenth century, by Cosimo himself and by his son Francesco I.

♦ **LIVORNO**
Under Cosimo I, work began on expanding the port of Livorno.

SIENA ♦
Giorgio Vasari made a wooden model of Siena for Cosimo I. It was useful in helping him decide how to besiege the city, which he intended to conquer.

♦ **MODELS**
During the Renaissance it became common practice for architects to make models of major building projects, in order to show their patrons how they intended to carry out their plans.

A PALACE AT AREZZO ♦
A model of a residence in Arezzo designed by Giorgio Vasari.

♦ Cosimo I's Academy

Cosimo I wanted the arts to serve the interests of the state. With this idea in mind, he founded the Accademia delle Arti del Disegno, later known as the Accademia di Belle Arti. The event is celebrated in this fresco by Bernardino Poccetti at the Loggiata degli Innocenti, Florence. The Accademia played an important part in consolidating Florence's influence on the arts, and in establishing Michelangelo's reputation as a great genius.

Giorgio Vasari ♦

One of the artists who best represented the idea of art in the service of the ducal court was Giorgio Vasari (1511-74). His most famous work is the Palazzo degli Uffizi, c.1560, the administrative headquarters of the Florentine state. The building later became one of the world's oldest art galleries.

♦ The Uffizi

Following the usual practice, Giorgio Vasari had a wooden model made of his project for the Palazzo degli Uffizi.

15. Michelangelo's life ♦ *Despite the resistance of many of its citizens, not least Michelangelo, Florence lost its republican freedoms in August 1530 and bowed again to Medici family rule. Fearful of the revenge that the ruthless Duke Alessandro might take on the defeated republicans, Michelangelo went into hiding until, from Rome, Clement VII issued an order that his life was to be spared. Michelangelo then returned to his work on the Medici tombs in the New Sacristy of San Lorenzo. In 1531, after the death of his father, he experienced difficulties in administering the property he had inherited. The following year he went to Rome, where he made new friends and was promised further commissions by Pope Paul III. After this he returned briefly to Florence and continued work on the New Sacristy, until the Pope unexpectedly summoned him to paint a vast fresco of the* Last Judgement *on the end wall of the Sistine Chapel. In 1534, perhaps glad to escape from the Medici, Michelangelo left his native city, never to return.* ➤

THE THEATRE AND LITERATURE

Sixteenth-century high culture was based on princely courts, and it was in this environment that the theatre and literary activities developed. In Florence, the Medici not only held spectacular celebrations for family occasions such as weddings and funerals, but also introduced an important innovation by staging an annual season of theatrical events. They employed artists who were kept busy designing scenery and costumes and devising entertainments of all kinds. But Michelangelo was not one of their number. He took little pleasure in such frivolous pastimes. In addition to his work as an artist, he wrote letters and poems (sonnets) of a serious nature. These activities were essentially private. His writings expressed his feelings and ideas, especially about religious subjects, and he preferred to share these only with a few intimate friends.

✦ VITTORIA COLONNA
Michelangelo met the noblewoman Vittoria Colonna in Rome in 1536 and she became one of his dearest friends, sharing his enthusiasms in religion, art and poetry. This portrait of her is attributed to Sebastiano del Piombo, c.1535 (Museo di Palazzo Venezia, Rome).

STANDS ✦
Watching from windows and balconies, the Medici and their guests enjoyed the spectacle as we might watch a play from a box in a modern theatre.

✦ BUONTALENTI
One of the first permanent theatres was constructed in the Palazzo degli Uffizi, c.1585, by Bernardo Buontalenti. This architect, sculptor and painter also designed scenery. The drawing on the left (Uffizi Gallery, Florence) is one of his stage-set designs.

✦ COSTUMES
Like many artists of the time, Buontalenti also devoted his attention to designing costumes for the theatre. He made this drawing of some costumes in 1589 (Biblioteca Nazionale, Florence).

✦ MICHELANGELO'S LONELINESS
Above: Giorgio Vasari, *Cosimo I and the Artists of his Court*, 1555-62 (Palazzo Vecchio, Florence). Though patronized by the Medici, Michelangelo distanced himself from court life. His letters tell of his loneliness as an artist. On 22 February 1556 he wrote to Vasari: "It has pleased God ... to let me live on in this fickle world with so many troubles ... and I can look forward to nothing but endless misery."

♦ **A SEA BATTLE**
A naval battle between Turks and Christians was staged in the courtyard of the Palazzo Pitti as part of the celebrations for the wedding of Ferdinando de' Medici and Christine of Lorraine, 11 May 1589.

♦ **SHIPS**
The courtyard of the palace was lined with waterproof materials and then flooded, to accommodate no fewer than eighteen galleys of various shapes and sizes.

THE LAST JUDGEMENT

The Gospel according to St Matthew records the
teachings of Jesus about the Last Judgement. He
warned of a time when Christ would return to Earth to
separate the Good from the Bad and send them to
Heaven or Hell. European artists from medieval times
onwards often pictured the Last Judgement, since it
was a subject of central importance for Christian
believers. Christ, in his role as judge, was normally
shown in the centre of the firmament, flanked by the
apostles, the Virgin Mary and the saints. Below, the
dead were shown rising from their tombs.

*Even more than in the
Sistine ceiling, the figures
and composition of the
Last Judgement reveal
Michelangelo's sculptural
conception of painting. It is
perhaps significant that he
began this fresco just
after he had been working
on the Medici tombs.*

*He did a great deal of
preparatory work for this
vast new undertaking:
drawings, studies and
cartoons. He also modified
the surface of the chapel
wall so that it sloped
slightly inward as it went
down, protecting it against
falling dust and dirt.*

♦ MOSAIC
An earlier example of
a *Last Judgement* is
the mosaic by the
workshop of Meliore,
c.1225 (detail below),
which decorates the
cupola of the
Baptistery in
Florence. The scene
is dominated by
Christ as judge.

♦ ST BARTHOLOMEW
One of the martyrs
portrayed in
Michelangelo's fresco
is St Bartholomew,
who was flayed alive.
With biting
humour, the artist
painted his own
face on the skin
that the saint is
displaying.

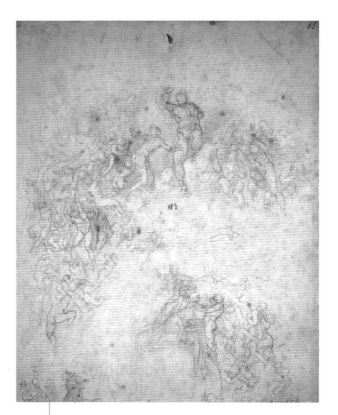

♦ A STUDY
In this drawing (Casa
Buonarroti, Florence),
Michelangelo was
working out how to
give his Christ a
dynamic force that
would make him the
focal point of the
whole composition.

♦ THE SAVED
According to the writings of St Augustine, on the Day of Judgement the dead will arise with bodies the age of the resurrected Christ (that is, thirty-three years old), regardless of their actual age when they died.

♦ THE COMPOSITION
Conceived as a single scene, the fresco has a clear arrangement. Christ the judge occupies the centre, and is surrounded by saints. Near him are the angels and the saved, who are shown floating up to heaven.

♦ SYMBOLISM
Angels carry the cross, the crown of thorns and the column to which Christ was tied for scourging.

ANGELS ♦
In the lower central area of the fresco, angels on a cloud blow trumpets to summon all humankind to judgement. The names of the saved are in the smaller of the two books.

CHARON ♦
Charon the ferryman discharges damned souls from his boat in the presence of Minos.

♦ MARTYRS
The Christian martyrs, bearing the symbols of their martyrdom, are represented in the middle section of the fresco. St Catherine, for instance, is shown holding her wheel.

MICHELANGELO IN ROME

From the fifteenth century, intent on restoring Rome to its former glory, the popes commissioned new building work in the city. The pace quickened as the political power of the papacy increased, and architects began to flock to the papal court. As a result, Rome became the centre of great new architectural projects and town planning schemes. Despite setbacks and disasters, including the sack of the city by the troops of Charles V in 1527, Rome continued to expand. Michelangelo finally settled in the city in 1534 and from then onwards he played a leading part in its artistic and cultural history. He not only produced masterpieces of painting and sculpture, but was also responsible for great building projects. From 1538 he planned a new layout and façades for the Piazza del Campidoglio. He redesigned and, from 1547, supervised the work on St Peter's. He erected a new city gate, the Porta Pia, built in 1561-64, and planned the conversion of the ancient baths of Diocletian into the church of Santa Maria degli Angeli.

♦ **BUILDING WORK IN THE PIAZZA**
This etching of c.1547, by Jeronymus Cock, shows building work in its early stages in the Piazza del Campidoglio. The ramp for the new set of steps on the right of the façade of the Palazzo del Senatore had not yet been constructed.

♦ **SANTA MARIA DEGLI ANGELI**
The great hall of the baths of Diocletian was consecrated for Christian worship in 1550 and was dedicated to Santa Maria degli Angeli. Michelangelo's plan to transform it into a church was approved in 1561.

16. MICHELANGELO'S LIFE ♦ *On arriving in Rome in September 1534, Michelangelo learned that Clement VII had died just a few days before. But Clement's successor, Paul III, was also an admirer of Michelangelo's work and confirmed the commission for the* Last Judgement. *So Michelangelo went back to live in his house in the Via Macel de' Corvi. During this period he mixed in Roman literary and intellectual circles, and his close friendship with the poet Vittoria Colonna strengthened his faith and intensified his preoccupation with religion. He was in his sixties when he worked on the* Last Judgement. *After one awkward fall on the scaffolding, he had to spend a month in bed recovering. As well as painting, he was still working on Julius II's tomb and also undertook a major architectural project: to provide new designs for the Piazza del Campidoglio. In 1547, he became the chief architect of St Peter's.* ➤+

♦ **PORTA PIA**
In 1561, Pius IV commissioned a gate in the city walls at the end of the Via Pia. The street, named after him, had already been laid out on his orders. The Porta Pia is an arched gateway, much as Michelangelo designed it, except for the pediment at the very top, which was added later.

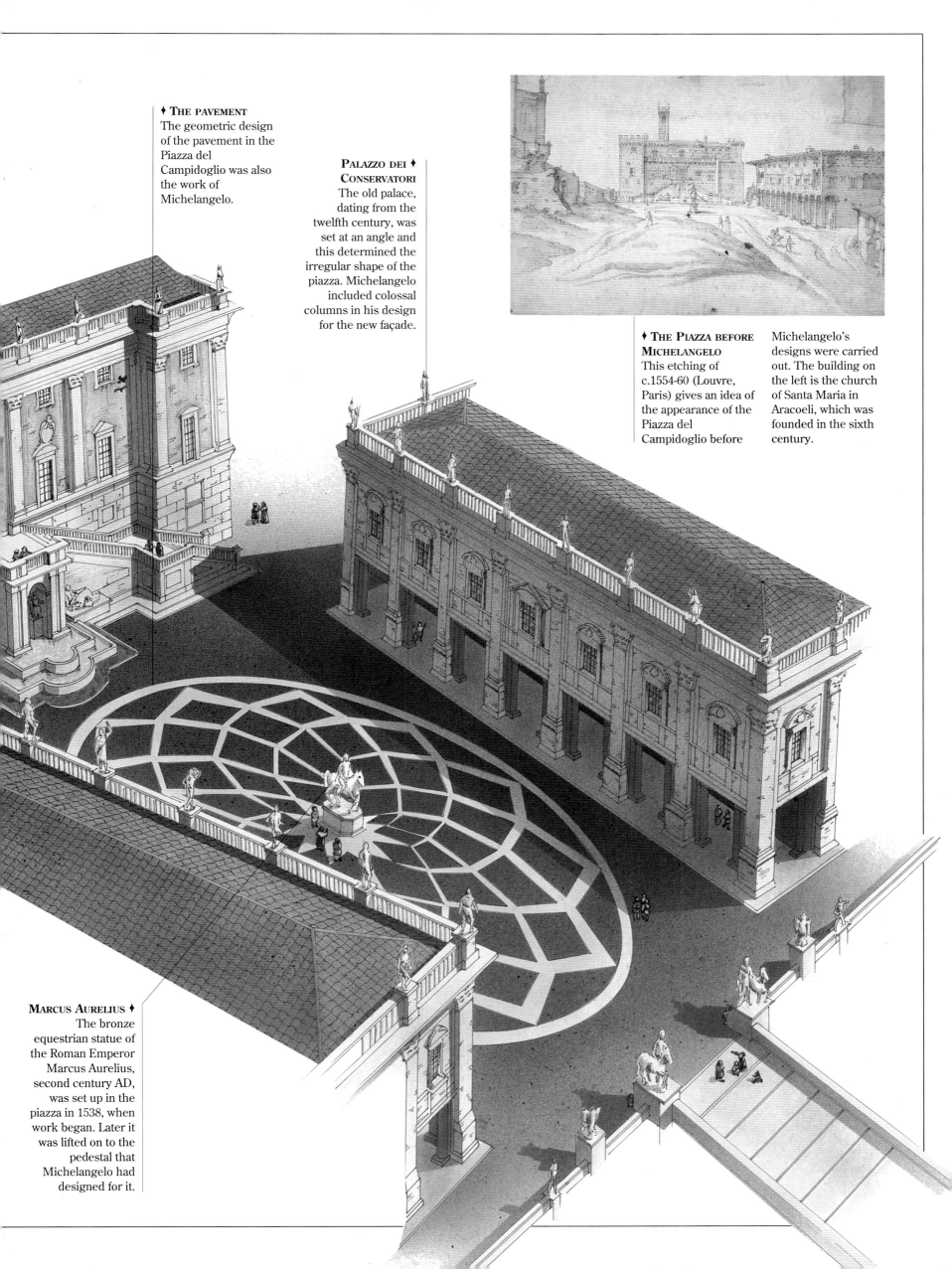

♦ **THE PAVEMENT**
The geometric design of the pavement in the Piazza del Campidoglio was also the work of Michelangelo.

PALAZZO DEI ♦ CONSERVATORI
The old palace, dating from the twelfth century, was set at an angle and this determined the irregular shape of the piazza. Michelangelo included colossal columns in his design for the new façade.

♦ **THE PIAZZA BEFORE MICHELANGELO**
This etching of c.1554-60 (Louvre, Paris) gives an idea of the appearance of the Piazza del Campidoglio before Michelangelo's designs were carried out. The building on the left is the church of Santa Maria in Aracoeli, which was founded in the sixth century.

MARCUS AURELIUS ♦
The bronze equestrian statue of the Roman Emperor Marcus Aurelius, second century AD, was set up in the piazza in 1538, when work began. Later it was lifted on to the pedestal that Michelangelo had designed for it.

ST PETER'S, ROME

Almost all of the great Renaissance architects who were active in Rome had a hand in the rebuilding of St Peter's: Bramante, Raphael, Antonio da Sangallo the Younger, Baldassare Peruzzi, and finally Michelangelo. When he took over, Michelangelo was constrained in his planning by the existence of building work already carried out by his predecessors. While he appreciated and retained some of Bramante's ideas, he was highly critical of da Sangallo's efforts. He made his dislike obvious to the contractors and administrators associated with da Sangallo, who were still engaged on the building, and they in turn put every possible obstacle in his way. However, his main preoccupation was the dome that was to crown the great church. In designing it, he drew inspiration from Brunelleschi's dome for Florence Cathedral. To demonstrate how the mighty structure was to be raised, he had a large wooden model made, of just half of the dome. After his death, the model was altered to show the modifications introduced by later architects in the final stages of the work.

♦ THE FINISHED CHURCH
Louis Haghe, *The Church of St Peter's, Rome, seen from the Square*, 1868 (Victoria and Albert Museum, London).

♦ CHIEF ARCHITECT OF ST PETER'S
After Bramante, Raphael, Antonio da Sangallo the Younger and Baldassare Peruzzi, it fell to Michelangelo to direct the building of St Peter's and organize the enormous construction site that had grown up around the church. He was appointed to the task in January 1547 by Pope Paul III. Now seventy-one, and feeling his age, he had been reluctant to take on so great a responsibility. In return, the Pope gave him a free hand in all matters and the sum of fifty *scudi* a month, although for Michelangelo the work was purely a labour of love. For the last eighteen years of his life, he devoted most of his efforts to this colossal project. Although he made the greatest single contribution to St Peter's, the church took centuries to complete. The dome, much altered from his design, was finished by Giacomo della Porta and Domenico Fontana. Above: a window in the drum of the dome.

♦ THE MODEL OF THE DOME
In 1558-61, to demonstrate his plans for the dome, Michelangelo made a 1:15 model from lime wood painted with tempera. It measures 5 x 4 x 2 metres (16 x 13 x 7 feet) and can still be seen in the Vatican today.

♦ PRESENTING THE MODEL
Michelangelo explains his plans for the dome to the Pope and his cardinals.

♦ **THE LANTERN**
The lantern on the model was altered after Michelangelo's death to show Giacomo della Porta's new design.

♦ **JOUSTING AT THE VATICAN**
This print by Jacob Binck, c.1565, shows the Belvedere courtyard being used for a knightly joust.

St Peter's can be seen in the background, on the right. Building work on the dome is in progress, with the drum almost finished.

♦ **INSPIRED BY BRUNELLESCHI**
Michelangelo took the idea of ribs from Brunelleschi's dome for Florence Cathedral.

♦ **THE INTERNAL DOME**
After Michelangelo's death, changes were made to his model of the dome. But the part showing the interior was left intact.

♦ **BRUNELLESCHI'S DOME**
It was from Brunelleschi's dome for Florence Cathedral, 1418-32, that Michelangelo took the idea of constructing a double vault, with an internal dome enclosed in an outer "shell". Brunelleschi's dome still showed the influence of Gothic architecture: the segments are rather angular and the white ribs stand out sharply against the red terracotta tiles. Simplicity and geometrical rigour characterize this early Renaissance masterpiece.

♦ **MICHELANGELO'S DOME**
The structure of Michelangelo's dome is hard to discern because of the wealth of decorative features he added to it. The drum is concealed by pairs of columns separating windows set beneath triangular or curved pediments. The segments of the dome, between the ribs, are embellished with small openings. As in the New Sacristy of San Lorenzo, Michelangelo effectively merged architecture and sculpture.

PIETÀS

A Pietà is a painting or sculpture showing the Virgin Mary supporting the body of the dead Christ in her lap, after he has been taken down from the cross. St John the Evangelist and Mary Magdalene are often present, and the group may include other persons such as Joseph or, as in the *Florence Pietà*, Nicodemus (a Pharisee who was present at Jesus's burial). Two other scenes closely related to that of a Pietà are also common in art: the Deposition, showing Jesus's body being taken down from the cross, and the Lamentation, in which his family and followers mourn over him.

♦ **THE FACE OF CHRIST**
A detail from the *Florence Pietà*, 1550-55.

♦ **FLORENCE PIETÀ**
Michelangelo, 1550-55; marble, 226 cm (89 in) high (Museo dell'Opera del Duomo, Florence). According to his biographers, Michelangelo intended this sculpture for his own tomb in Santa Maria Maggiore in Rome. In the event, he sold it in 1561 and it came into the hands of Tiberio Calcagni, who made some major alterations to the original work. The sculpture was transported to Florence in 1674, on the orders of Grand Duke Cosimo III, and set up in San Lorenzo, the Medici family church. In 1721, it was moved to the cathedral, where it stood behind the high altar. Recently, for security reasons, the Pietà has been moved again, to the nearby Museo dell'Opera dell'Duomo.

♦ **IN THE CATHEDRAL**
A nineteenth-century print shows the position of the Pietà in Florence Cathedral.

RONDANINI PIETÀ ♦
This was the last Pietà carved by Michelangelo, 1552-64 (Castello Sforzesco, Milan).

STUDY ♦
Michelangelo made this drawing representing the dead Christ (Louvre, Paris), to help his colleague Sebastiano del Piombo. It was rare for Michelangelo to produce such a highly finished drawing. It demonstrates his thorough understanding of human anatomy.

The Florence Pietà *was repaired and worked on by Tiberio Calcagni, after Michelangelo had mutilated and discarded it. Calcagni finished the figure of Mary Magdalene, which Michelangelo had merely roughed out, giving it a more polished appearance than the others in the group. He restored the left leg of Christ, which Michelangelo had broken off – and which was later removed again. His intervention can also be seen in the face of Mary. The composition of the piece is quite different from that of Michelangelo's other three Pietàs, since here the group forms a pyramid.*

♦ VATICAN PIETÀ

This is the first and most traditional of Michelangelo's four Pietàs, with the Virgin supporting the limp body of Christ across her knees. It dates from 1498-1500 (St Peter's, Rome).

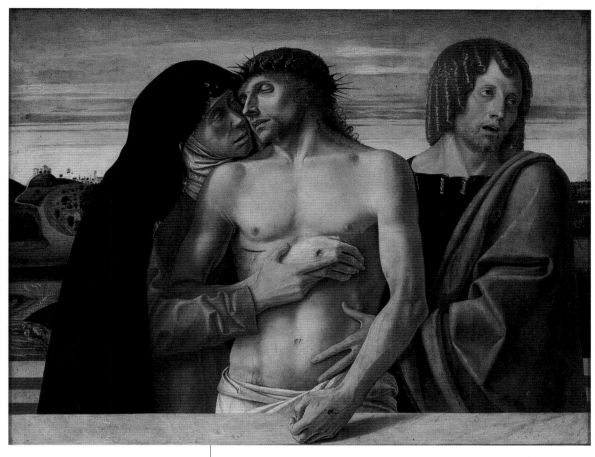

GIOTTO ♦

Mary's grief after the death of Christ became a common theme of European art in the thirteenth century. Giotto took the subject for one of his frescos in the Scrovegni Chapel in Padua. His originality lay in representing sacred events in human terms, as in the *Lamentation*, 1302-06.

GIOVANNI BELLINI ♦

In Bellini's *Lament over the Body of Christ*, 1460 (Brera, Milan), the figures are shown half-length, behind a marble sill. Bellini painted this subject several times.

♦ PALESTRINA PIETÀ

One of Michelangelo's last works, 1550-59 (Galleria dell'Accademia, Florence). The dramatic tension and rough-hewn effect of the carving make a powerful impression.

MICHELANGELO'S LEGACY

As early as 1520, many Italians had come to believe that art had reached perfection in the works of Michelangelo, Raphael, Leonardo da Vinci and Titian, and that the beauty and harmony they had achieved could never be bettered. The painter Giorgio Vasari, who wrote the first collection of artists' biographies, was particularly insistent on the superiority of the Renaissance. When younger contemporaries of the great masters tried to follow in their footsteps, they tended to imitate or exaggerate their manner – hence the name Mannerists, applied to many late sixteenth-century Italian painters. Others sought to distinguish themselves by straining after originality. But even their efforts can usually be traced back to innovations first introduced by Michelangelo.

♦ **COSIMO I**
A detail from Vasari's *Cosimo I and the Artists of his Court* (Palazzo Vecchio, Florence).

♦ **BACK IN FLORENCE**
The period following Michelangelo's departure for Rome in 1534 was marked by the ascendancy of the Medici, who now exercised absolute power. Art became an instrument of political control, with artists working mainly in the service of the Medici dukes. When Cosimo I was raised to the rank of Grand Duke, the state of Tuscany became a force to be reckoned with. In sculpture, Michelangelo's followers tended to focus on one aspect of his art: the sense of the colossal, the heroic and the awesome. But their interpretations were often pompous and lacking in inspiration. Among Michelangelo's would-be imitators were Baccio Bandinelli (Florence, 1493-1560), a great favourite of the Medici; Bartolomeo Ammanati (Settignano, 1511 – Florence, 1592), who also assisted the more distinguished Sansovino in Venice; and Bernardo Buontalenti (Florence, 1536-1608), a pupil of Vasari. Two highly original artists working in Florence in the second half of the sixteenth century were Benvenuto Cellini (Florence, 1500-71) and the French sculptor Jean de Boulogne, known as Giambologna (Douai, 1529 – Florence, 1608).

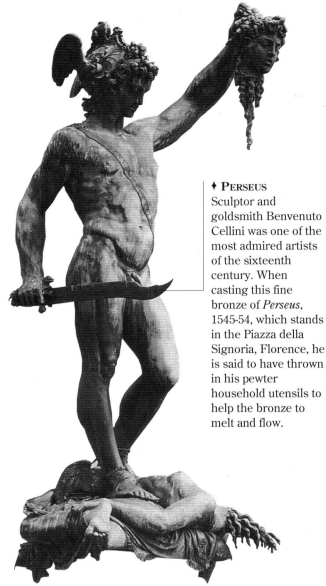

♦ **PERSEUS**
Sculptor and goldsmith Benvenuto Cellini was one of the most admired artists of the sixteenth century. When casting this fine bronze of *Perseus*, 1545-54, which stands in the Piazza della Signoria, Florence, he is said to have thrown in his pewter household utensils to help the bronze to melt and flow.

♦ **HERCULES AND CACUS**
Baccio Bandinelli, one of Michelangelo's best-known rivals, carved this marble group of *Hercules and Cacus*, 1534, for the Piazza della Signoria, Florence, hoping that it would be thought the equal of the *David*.

NEPTUNE ♦
Bartolomeo Ammanati's statue of *Neptune*, 1563-77, for the Piazza della Signoria, Florence, did not find favour with the Florentines, who nicknamed it "il Biancone" (the big white lump). As with *Hercules and Cacus*, the style of this work derived from Michelangelo's *David*.

♦ BUONTALENTI
An eccentric artist and brilliant inventor in the service of the Medici, Buontalenti excelled as a military and civil engineer, stage designer and organizer of extravaganzas. The Porta delle Suppliche for the Uffizi, c.1580, with its reversed broken pediment, is one of his most unconventional works.

NARCISSUS ♦
Benvenuto Cellini, 1548 (Museo del Bargello, Florence). The pose of Cellini's *Narcissus*, the beautiful youth who fell in love with his own reflection, is typical of the late Renaissance in its rather self-conscious virtuosity.

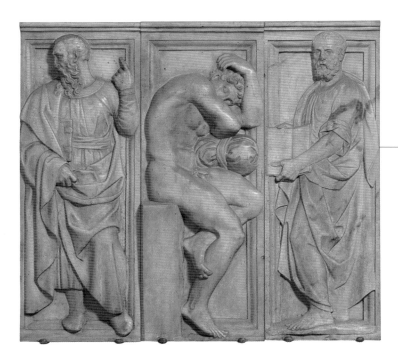

♦ CATHEDRAL CHOIR STALLS
In this relief work for the choir of Florence Cathedral, 1555, Baccio Bandinelli was using sculptures by Michelangelo as his model. This is particularly obvious in the powerful muscles and the pose of the sleeping nude figure in the centre.

♦ WINGED MERCURY
This bronze was made by Giambologna for Cosimo I, 1564-65 (Museo del Bargello, Florence). It represents the messenger of the gods in flight, transported on a puff of wind, which is shown issuing from the mouth of Zephyr, the figure at his feet. Introducing Zephyr was a clever way of giving the flying figure of Mercury something to stand on.

COMMEMORATING ♦ MICHELANGELO
After Michelangelo's death, the Accademia del Disegno held a ceremony to commemorate him, in the church of San Lorenzo. The church and the funding for the ceremony were made available by Cosimo I, though he did not himself take part in the occasion.
Right: Agostino Ciampelli, *The Memorial Service of Michelangelo*, 1617 (Casa Buonarroti, Florence).

17. MICHELANGELO'S LIFE ♦ *During his last years in Rome, Michelangelo carved three Pietàs, returning to a theme that had first attracted him in his youth when he produced the* Vatican Pietà. *The approach of death and his deepening religious convictions seem to have led him to dwell on the subject of Christ crucified and the grief of his family and friends. He also continued to work on the dome of St Peter's, striving to advance his plans as far as possible. He performed many charitable works and looked after his relatives in Florence, particularly his nephew Leonardo. Despite his advanced age, he remained active until the last days of his life. He died on 18 February 1564, having taken to his bed three days before. He was eighty-eight. His remains were taken to Florence, which he had not seen for thirty years, and were buried in the church of Santa Croce. At a memorial service in San Lorenzo, the Florentine Academy of Painters honoured Michelangelo's achievement.*

◆ KEY DATES IN MICHELANGELO'S LIFE

1475	Michelangelo is born on 6 March at Caprese, near Arezzo, second of the five sons of Lodovico Buonarroti, magistrate of Chiusi and Caprese, and of Francesca di Neri.
1488	Overcoming his father's opposition, Michelangelo joins the workshop of the celebrated Florentine painter Ghirlandaio, as apprentice-assistant.
1489	He leaves Ghirlandaio's workshop and begins to study sculpture in the school set up in the garden of Lorenzo the Magnificent near the Piazza San Marco in Florence.
1492	He finishes his relief sculpture of the *Battle of the Centaurs*. On Lorenzo's death, he leaves the Palazzo Medici and returns to his father's house.
1494	Charles VIII of France enters the Italian peninsula. The Medici take flight from Florence, and the city becomes a republic.
1496	In May Michelangelo makes his first visit to Rome, where Cardinal Riario becomes his patron. He begins work on his statue of *Bacchus*.
1501	Florence Cathedral works department entrusts Michelangelo with a huge block of marble from which to create a monumental statue of *David*.
1505	Pope Julius II commissions Michelangelo to make him a tomb. This ambitious project undergoes many changes over the years.
1508	After a brief stay in Florence, Michelangelo returns to Rome where Julius II commissions him to decorate the ceiling of the Sistine Chapel.
1516	The new pope, Leo X, a Florentine of the Medici family, commissions Michelangelo to design a façade for the church of San Lorenzo in Florence.
1519	Still employed by Leo X, Michelangelo begins designing the New Sacristy of San Lorenzo, a chapel to house the Medici tombs.
1523	Leo X's successor, Clement VII, another Medici pope, confirm's Michelangelo's commission to work on the church of San Lorenzo in Florence.
1527	The troops of Charles V sack Rome. The Medici are again expelled from Florence and Michelangelo's work on San Lorenzo is interrupted.
1528	Florence is threatened by the armies of Charles V. Michelangelo supervises the fortifications of the city, which is besieged and falls in 1530.
1534	Michelangelo moves permanently to Rome. He takes up his work on Julius II's tomb and is contracted to paint the *Last Judgement* in the Sistine Chapel.
1536	He begins work on his fresco of the *Last Judgement*. (Paul III has confirmed the original commission of the previous pope, Clement VII.)
1541	Michelangelo obtains permission to have Julius II's tomb completed by other sculptors working under his supervision.
1545	The tomb is finished: the final statues are set up in their architectural setting in the church of San Pietro in Vincoli, Rome.
1547	Pope Paul III appoints Michelangelo chief architect in charge of the new church of St Peter's, begun forty years earlier.
1561	Michelangelo presents the Pope with a large wooden model showing his design for the dome of St Peter's. His plans to transform the Baths of Diocletian into a church are approved.
1564	The church authorities decide to have parts of the *Last Judgement* covered up, on grounds of indecency. Michelangelo dies in Rome on 18 February. He is buried in Florence.

◆ CATALOGUE RAISONNÉ

As he said himself, Michelangelo was first and foremost a sculptor. He produced more work in this field than in architecture and painting, and was better able to express himself in this medium than in any other.

Fundamental to all his work was drawing. He used drawing to formulate his ideas before giving them expression in sculpture, painting or architecture. Many of his sketches and plans have survived.

His first works were sculptures in marble, and he always preferred this material. For him, sculpture was a matter of carving, rather than modelling or casting in bronze. Marble and stone are the materials he used for almost all his works of sculpture and architecture. Most of the latter are in Rome.

In the field of architecture, Michelangelo brought a sculptural quality to the buildings he designed. In Rome, in the last years of his life, he also undertook a great town planning project.

He was less active as a painter. He worked on only two or three paintings that were not done on a wall or ceiling. His frescos for the Vatican chapels were his greatest achievements.

SCULPTURE

Madonna of the Stairs, 1490-92 (Casa Buonarroti, Florence)
Battle of the Centaurs, c.1492 (Casa Buonarroti, Florence)
Sculptures for the shrine of St Dominic, 1494-95 (San Domenico, Bologna)
Bacchus, 1496-97 (Museo del Bargello, Florence)
Vatican Pietà, 1498-1500 (St Peter's, Rome)
Madonna and Child, c.1501 (Notre-Dame, Bruges)
David, 1501-04 (Galleria dell'Accademia, Florence)
Pitti Tondo, 1504-05 (Museo del Bargello, Florence)
Taddei Tondo, 1505-06 (Royal Academy of Fine Arts, London)
St Matthew, c.1505 (Galleria dell'Accademia, Florence)
Dying Slave, c.1513 (Louvre, Paris)
Rebel Slave, c.1513 (Louvre, Paris)
Moses, c.1515 (San Pietro in Vincoli, Rome)
Young Slave, 1513-20 (Galleria dell'Accademia, Florence)
Bearded Slave, 1513-20 (Galleria dell'Accademia, Florence)
Atlas, 1513-20 (Galleria dell'Accademia, Florence)
Awakening Slave, 1513-20 (Galleria dell'Accademia, Florence)
Medici tombs, 1524-34 (New Sacristy of San Lorenzo, Florence)
Tomb of Pope Julius II, 1505-42 (San Pietro in Vincoli, Rome)
Florence Pietà, 1550-55 (Museo dell'Opera del Duomo, Florence)
Palestrina Pietà, 1550-59 (Galleria dell'Accademia, Florence)
Rondanini Pietà, 1552-64 (Castello Sforzesco, Milan)

ARCHITECTURE

New Sacristy of San Lorenzo, Florence, 1524-34
Laurentian Library, Florence, 1524-34
Piazza del Campidoglio, Rome, c.1538-64
Palazzo Farnese, Rome, c.1546
Church and dome of St Peter's, Rome, c.1547-64
San Giovanni dei Fiorentini, Rome, c.1560
Santa Maria degli Angeli, Rome, 1561
Porta Pia, Rome, c.1561

PAINTING

Doni Tondo, c.1506 (Uffizi Gallery, Florence)
* *Madonna and Child, with the Infant St John and Angels* (*The Manchester Madonna*), 1498-1500 (National Gallery, London)
* *The Entombment*, c.1508 (National Gallery, London)

* These two paintings were unfinished and their attribution to Michelangelo is disputed.

Biblical Stories and Figures, 1508-12 (Sistine Chapel ceiling, Vatican, Rome)
Last Judgement, 1536-41 (Sistine Chapel, Vatican, Rome)
Conversion of St Paul, 1542-45 (Capella Paolina, Vatican, Rome)
Crucifixion of St Peter, 1542-45 (Capella Paolina, Vatican, Rome)

♦ LIST OF WORKS INCLUDED IN THIS BOOK

(Works reproduced in their entirety are indicated with the letter E; those of which only a detail is featured are followed by the letter D.)

The works reproduced in this book are listed here, with (when known) their date, their dimensions, the place they are currently housed, and the page number. The numbers in bold type refer to the credits on page 64. Abbreviation: MNB, Museo Nazionale del Bargello, Florence.

Anonymous
1 *Bacchus with Satyr*, Roman copy of a Greek original, marble (Museo Chiaramonti, Vatican Museums, Rome) 21 E; **2** *Battle of the Centaurs*, 5th century BC, fragment of marble frieze from the temple of Apollo at Bassae in Arcadia, Greece (British Museum, London) 15 D; **3** *Battle Scene*, 3rd century AD, marble relief on sarcophagus (Museo delle Terme, Rome) 15 D; **4** *Belvedere Apollo*, 2nd century AD, Roman copy of a Greek original, marble, 224 cm (88 in) high (Museo Pio-Clementino, Vatican Museums, Rome) 29 E; **5** *The Burning of Savonarola in the Piazza della Signoria*, 1498, tempera on panel, 101 x 115 cm (40 x 45 in) (Museo di San Marco, Florence) 17 E; **6** *Centaur*, 2nd century AD, sardonyx cameo, 5 x 4.2 cm (2 x 2 in) (Museo Nazionale, Naples) 14 E; **7** *Faun*, Roman copy of a Greek original, marble (Museo Pio-Clementino, Vatican Museums, Rome) 21 E; **8** *Florence*, 15th-century miniature, 33.3 x 22.5 cm (13 x 9 in) (from *Storia Fiorentina dall'Origine della Città fino all'Anno 1455* by Poggio Bracciolini, Vatican Library, Rome) 13 D; **9** *Venus Felix*, Roman copy of a Greek original, marble (Cortile Ottagono, Vatican Museums, Rome) 29 E; **10** *View of the Piazza del Campidoglio, Rome*, 1554-60, etching, 28 x 42 cm (11 x 17 in) (Louvre, Paris) 55 E

Agesander, Athenodorus, Polydorus
11 *Laocoön*, 2nd-1st century BC, marble, 245 cm (96 in) high (Museo Pio-Clementino, Vatican Museums, Rome) 29 E, 30 E

Ammanati, Bartolomeo
12 *Neptune*, 1563-77, marble statue for marble and bronze fountain, 560 cm (220 in) high (Piazza della Signoria, Florence) 60 E

Antonello da Messina
13 *St Jerome in his Study*, 1474, oil on panel, 46 x 36.5 cm (18 x 14 in) (National Gallery, London) 10 E

Apollonius of Athens
14 *Belvedere Torso*, 1st century BC, marble, 195 cm (77 in) high (Museo Pio-Clementino, Vatican Museums, Rome) 29 E

Bandinelli, Baccio
16 *Hercules and Cacus*, 1534, marble, c.496 cm (195 in) high (Piazza della Signoria, Florence) 60 E; **17** Relief with *Sleeping Nude*, 1555 (Museo dell'Opera del Duomo, Florence) 61 E

Bartolomeo, Fra
17 *Portrait of Girolamo Savonarola*, early 15th century, oil on panel (Museo di San Marco, Florence) 16 E

Bellini, Giovanni
18 *Lament over the Body of Christ*, 1460, tempera on panel, 86 x 107 cm (34 x 42 in) (Brera, Milan) 59 E

Bertoldo di Giovanni
19 *Apollo*, mid-15th century, bronze, 43.7 cm (17 in) high (MNB) 7 E; **20** *Battle Scene*, mid-15th century, bronze relief, 45 x 99 cm (18 x 39 in) (MNB) 15 E; **21** *Hercules* (attr.), 1470-75, bronze, 49 cm (19 in) high (Victoria and Albert Museum, London) 24 E; **22** *Young Man with Medallion of Plato's "Chariot of the Soul"* (attr.), 1440, bronze bust (MNB) 12 D

Binck, Jacob
23 *Joust in the Belvedere Courtyard of the Vatican*, c.1565, etching 57 E

Botticelli, Sandro (and workshop)
24 *Portrait of Young Woman*, 1483, tempera on panel, 82 x 54 cm (32 x 21 in) (Kunstinstitut Gemäldegalerie, Frankfurt) 12 E

Bronzino, Agnolo
25 *Holy Family with the Infant St John (Holy Family Panciatichi)*, 1540, oil on panel, 117 x 93 cm (46 x 36 in) (Uffizi, Florence) 31 E; **26** *Portrait of Clement VII*, 1553, oil on metal, 15 x 12 cm (6 x 5 in) (Uffizi, Florence) 33 E

Bronzino, Agnolo (workshop of)
27 *Portrait of Piero II de' Medici*, 1553, oil on metal, 15 x 12 cm (6 x 5 in) (Uffizi, Florence) 17 E

Buontalenti, Bernardo
28 Costume sketches for *La Pellegrina*, 1589 (Biblioteca Nazionale, Florence) 50 E; **29** Sketch for a stage-set with buildings in perspective, late 16th century (Uffizi, Florence) 50 E

Cartari, Vincenzo
30 *Bacchus*, 1556 (from *Le Imagine degli Dèi Antichi*) 20 E

Cellini, Benvenuto
31 *Cosimo I*, 1545, bronze bust with traces of gilding, 134.8 x 98 cm (53 x 39 in) (MNB) 48 E; **32** *Narcissus*, 1548, marble, 35 cm (14 in) high (MNB) 61 E; **33** *Perseus*, 1545-54, bronze on marble base, 320 cm (126 in) high (Loggia dei Lanzi, Piazza della Signoria, Florence) 60 E

Ciampelli, Agostino
34 *The Memorial Service of Michelangelo*, 1617, oil on canvas (Casa Buonarroti, Florence) 61 E

Cock, Jeronymus
35 *View of the Piazza del Campidoglio, Rome*, c.1547, etching (British Museum, London) 54 E

De Greyss, Benedetto Vincenzo
36 *Michelangelo's Bacchus at the Uffizi*, c.1750 (from the *Inventario Illustrato della Galleria degli Uffizi*) (Uffizi, Florence) 21 E

Donatello, byname of Niccolò di Betto Bardi
37 *David*, c.1430-33, bronze, 158 cm (62 in) high (MNB) 25 E; **38** *Madonna and Child (Piot Madonna)* (attr.), c.1460, terracotta with traces of gilding, inlaid with glass, 74 x 75 x 7 cm (29 x 30 x 3 in) (Louvre, Paris) 7 E; **39** *St George*, 1416-20, marble, 209 cm (82 in) high (MNB) 6 E, 26 D

Ferrucci, Andrea
40 *Marsilio Ficino*, 1522, bronze bust (Florence Cathedral) 12 E

Fontebuoni, Anastasio
41 *Michelangelo in Conversation with Pope Julius II*, 1620-21 (Casa Buonarroti, Florence) 33 E

Furini, Francesco
42 *Lorenzo the Magnificent surrounded by artists*, 1636, fresco (Palazzo Pitti, Florence) 10 E

Ghirlandaio, Domenico
43 Study for *The Marriage of the Virgin*, c.1485, pen and ink drawing, 20.1 x 26.3 cm (8 x 10 in) (Uffizi, Florence) 8 E

Giambologna, byname of Jean de Boulogne
44 *Mercury*, 1564-65, bronze, 100 cm (39 in) high (MNB) 61 E

Giotto
45 *The Ascension of St John*, 1315-20, fresco (Santa Croce, Florence) 10 E; **46** *Lamentation*, 1302-06, fresco (Scrovegni Chapel, Padua) 59 E

Giulio Romano
47 *Aristocratic Banquet*, c.1526, fresco (Venus and Psyche Room, Palazzo del Tè, Mantua) 36 E

Granacci, Francesco
48 *Charles VIII entering Florence*, early 16th century, tempera on panel, 76 x 122 cm (30 x 48 in) (Uffizi, Florence) 16 E

Haghe, Louis
49 *The Church of St Peter's, Rome, seen from the Square*, 1868 (Victoria and Albert Museum, London) 56 E

Heemskerck, Martin van
50 *Michelangelo's Bacchus in the Garden of Jacopo Galli*, 1533, etching (Kupferstichkabinett, Berlin) 21 E

Levasseur, Jean-Charles
51 *Michelangelo's Pietà in Florence Cathedral*, 19th century, lithograph, 31 x 24.8 cm (12 x 10 in) (Museo di Firenze com'era, Florence) 58 D

Mantegna, Andrea
52 *Bacchanalia with Wine-Vat*, 1470-90, etching, 33.5 x 45.4 cm (13 x 18 in) (Uffizi, Florence) 21 E

Masaccio, byname of Tommaso Cassai
53 *The Expulsion of Adam and Eve from the Earthly Paradise*, c.1425, fresco, 208 x 88 cm (82 x 35 in) (Brancacci Chapel, Santa Maria del Carmine, Florence) 11 E; **54** *The Tribute Money*, c.1425, fresco, 225 x 598 cm (89 x 235 in) (Brancacci Chapel, Santa Maria del Carmine, Florence) 10 E

Masolino da Panicale
55 *Adam and Eve before their Expulsion*, c.1424, fresco, 208 x 88 cm (82 x 35 in) (Brancacci Chapel, Santa Maria del Carmine, Florence) 11 E

Meliore (workshop of)
56 *Christ Pantocrator*, c.1225, mosaic (Baptistery, Florence) 52 D

Michelangelo Buonarroti
57 Anatomical study for a human figure, 1508-12, sanguine, 40.6 x 20.7 cm (16 x 8 in) (British Library, London) 9 E; **58** *Atlas*, 1513-20, marble, 277 cm (109 in) high (Galleria dell'Accademia, Florence) 26 D, 27 E; **59** *Awakening Slave*, 1513-20, marble, 267 cm (105 in) high (Galleria dell'Accademia, Florence) 27 E; **60** *Bacchus*, 1496-97, marble, 184 cm (72 in) high (MNB) 20 E; **61** *Battle of the Centaurs*, 1492, marble relief, 84.5 x 90.5 cm (33 x 36 in) (Casa Buonarroti, Florence) 14 E, D; **62** *Bearded Slave*, 1513-20, marble, 263 cm (104 in) high (Galleria dell'Accademia, Florence) 27 E; **63** *Caricature of himself painting the Sistine Ceiling*, 1508-12, pen and ink in the margin of a sonnet written in Rome (Casa Buonarroti, Florence) 37 E; **64** *Ceiling of the Sistine Chapel*, 1508-12, frescos, 13 x 36 m (43 x 118 ft) (Vatican Palaces, Rome) 30 D, 38-39 D, 40 D, 41 D [Caryatid *putti* 41; *The Creation of Adam* 38 D; *The Delphic Sibyl* 30; *The Fall and the Expulsion from Eden* 39 E; Imitation bronze medallion with *The Destruction of the Tribe of Ahab* 38 E; *The Libyan Sibyl* 40; Lunette of *Hezekiah, Manasseh, Amon* 39 D; *Male nudes* 41; *The Prophet Jeremiah* 40; Spandrel above lunette of *Jesse, David, Solomon* 40 D]; **65** Compositional study for the *Last Judgement*, c.1536, charcoal and sanguine, 41.5 x 29.8 cm (16 x 12 in) (Casa Buonarroti, Florence) 52 E; **66** *David*, 1501-04, marble, 410 cm (161 in) high (Galleria dell'Accademia, Florence) 24 E, D; **67** *Dying Slave*, c.1513, marble, 229 cm (90 in) high (Louvre, Paris) 35 E; **68** *Florence Pietà*, c.1550-55, marble, 226 cm (89 in) high (Museo dell'Opera del Duomo, Florence) 58 E; **69** *Holy Family with the Infant St John (Doni Tondo)*, c.1506, tempera on panel, 120 cm (47 in) diameter (Uffizi, Florence) 30 E; **70** *Last Judgement*, 1536-41, fresco, 13.7 x 12.2 m (45 x 40 ft) (Sistine Chapel, Vatican Palaces, Rome) 52 D, 53 E; **71** *Madonna and Child (Medici Madonna)*, c.1521, marble, 226 cm (89 in) high (New Sacristy, San Lorenzo, Florence) 26 E; **72** Model for the façade of San Lorenzo, Florence, c.1518, wood, 216 x 283 x 50 cm (85 x 111 x 20 in) (Casa Buonarroti, Florence) 43; **73** *Palestrina Pietà*, c.1550-59, marble, 263 cm (104 in) (Galleria dell'Accademia, Florence) 59 E; **74** Plan of bastions for a gate, 1528, pen and brown wash, 29.3 x 41.2 cm (12 x 16 in) (Casa Buonarroti, Florence) 46 E; **75** *Portrait of Andrea Quaratesi*, 1530-40, charcoal, 41.1 x 29.2 cm (16 x 11 in) (British Museum, London) 8 E; **76** *Rebel Slave*, c.1513, marble, 215 cm (85 in) high (Louvre, Paris) 35 E; **77** *Rondanini Pietà*, 1552-64, marble, 195 cm (77 in) high (Castello Sforzesco, Milan) 26 D, 58 E; **78** Sketches of blocks for the façade of San Lorenzo, Florence, 1521, pen, 20.4 x 30.3 cm (8 x 12 in) (Casa Buonarroti, Florence) 34 E; **79** *St Peter*, copied from Masaccio's *Tribute Money*, c.1490, pen and sanguine on white paper, 39.5 x 19.7 cm (16 x 8 in) (Graphische Sammlungen, Munich) 10 E; **80** Study of the *Belvedere Apollo*, sanguine (Louvre, Paris) 28 E; **81** Study for a door at the head of the staircase of the Laurentian Library, Florence, 1526, charcoal, pen and wash, 40.5 x 25.3 cm (16 x 10 in) (Casa Buonarroti, Florence) 6 E; **82** Study for a Pietà, 1533, charcoal, 25.4 x 31.8 cm (10 x 13 in) (Louvre, Paris) 58 E; **83** Study for the arm of *David*, 1501-04, pen on paper, 26.5 x 18.7 cm (10 x 7 in) (Louvre, Paris) 25 E; **84** Study for the *Tomb of Pope Julius II*, 1513, charcoal, pen and wash, fragment, 29 x 36.1 cm (11 x 14 in) (Uffizi, Florence) 35 E; **85** *Tomb of Giuliano de' Medici, Duke of Nemours*, 1524-34, marble, 6.3 x 4.2 m (21 x 14 ft) (New Sacristy, San Lorenzo, Florence) 44 D, E, 45 D; **86** *Tomb of Lorenzo de' Medici, Duke of Urbino*, 1524-34, marble, 6.3 x 4.2 m (21 x 14 ft) (New Sacristy, San Lorenzo, Florence) 44 D, 45 E; **87** *Tomb of Pope Julius II*, 1512-45, marble, 7 x 6.9 m (23 x 23 ft) (San Pietro in Vincoli, Rome) 35 E; **88** Two male figures, copy of Giotto's *Ascension of St John*, c.1490, pen on white paper, 31.7 x 20.4 cm (12 x 8 in) (Louvre, Paris) 10 E; **89** *Young Slave*, 1513-20, marble, 256 cm (101 in) high (Galleria dell'Accademia, Florence) 27 E; **90** *Vatican Pietà*, 1498-1500, marble, 174 cm (69 in) high (St Peter's, Rome) 26 D, 59 E

Michelozzo (workshop of)
91 *Tondo with Centaur*, 15th century, relief (courtyard of Palazzo Medici Riccardi, Florence) 14 E

Palma Vecchio, byname of Jacopo Negretti
92 *Holy Family with the Infant St John and Mary Magdalene*, 1508-12, oil on panel, 87 x 117 cm (34 x 46 in) (Uffizi, Florence) 31 E

Piero di Cosimo
93 *Battle of Lapiths and Centaurs*, late 15th century, oil on panel, 71 x 260 cm (28 x 102 in) (National Gallery, London) 15 E

Poccetti, Bernardino
94 *Cosimo I instituting the Accademia del Disegno*, early 17th century, fresco (Loggiato degli Innocenti, Florence) 49 E; **95** *Pier Capponi tearing up the Agreement with Charles VIII*, 1583-86, fresco (Reception Room, Palazzo Capponi, Florence) 17 E

Pollaiuolo, Antonio
96 *Niccolò Machiavelli*, late 15th century, marble bust (MNB) 23 E

Raphael
97 *Portrait of Agnolo Doni*, 1506, oil on panel, 63 x 45 cm (25 x 18 in) (Galleria Palatina, Palazzo Pitti, Florence) 30 E; **98** *Portrait of Maddalena Strozzi*, 1506, oil on panel, 63 x 45 cm (25 x 18 in) (Galleria Palatina, Palazzo Pitti, Florence) 30 E; **99** *Portrait of Julius II*, 1512, tempera on panel, 108.5 x 80 cm (43 x 31 in) (Uffizi, Florence) 32 E; **100** *Portrait of Leo X with Cardinals Luigi de' Rossi and Giulio de' Medici*, 1518, tempera on panel, 155.5 x 119.5 cm (61 x 47 in) (Uffizi, Florence) 32 D; **101** *The School of Athens*, 1508-11, fresco (Stanza della Segnatura, Vatican Palaces, Rome) 32-33 E, 32 D

Raphael (workshop of)
102 Grotesque decoration for the Stufetta (bathroom) of Cardinal Bibbiena, 1516, fresco paintings (Vatican Palaces, Rome) 36

Rosselli, Matteo
103 *Michelangelo as Commissioner for Fortifications*, 1615, oil on canvas (Casa Buonarroti, Florence) 47 E

Rossellino, Bernardo
104 *Tomb of Leonardo Bruni*, 1446-50, partly gilded marble, 7.2 m (23 ft) high (Santa Croce, Florence) 19 D

Sansovino, Jacopo
105 *Bacchus with Satyr*, c.1514, marble, 146 cm (57 in) high (MNB) 20 E

Sebastiano del Piombo, byname of Sebastiano Luciani
106 *Portrait of Vittoria Colonna*, c.1535, oil on panel, 69 x 54 cm (27 x 21 in) (Museo di Palazzo Venezia, Rome) 50 E

Signorelli, Luca
107 *Holy Family*, 1490-91, tempera on panel, 124 cm (49 in) diameter (Uffizi, Florence) 31 E

Titian
108 *The Emperor Charles V of Habsburg on Horseback*, 1548, oil on canvas, 3.3 x 2.8 m (11 x 9 ft) (Prado, Madrid) 47 D; **109** *Portrait of Pope Paul III with his nephews Cardinals Alessandro and Ottavio Farnese*, 1546, oil on canvas, 210 x 174 cm (82 x 69 in) (Galleria Nazionale, Naples) 33 D

Tribolo, Niccolò
110 *Fiesole*, allegorical statue for a fountain at the Medici Villa, Castello, Florence, early 16th century, marble (MNB) 19 E

Utens, Giusto
111 *Medici Villa, Poggio a Caiano*, late 16th century, tempera on canvas, 143 x 285 cm (56 x 112 in) (Museo di Firenze com'era, Florence) 19 E

Vasari, Giorgio
112 *The Arrival of Leo X in Florence*, 1555-62, fresco (Leo X apartment, Palazzo Vecchio, Florence) 25 E; **113** *Cosimo I and the Artists of his Court*, 1555-62, fresco (Palazzo Vecchio, Florence) 50 E, 60 D; **114** *Portrait of Lorenzo de' Medici*, 1488-90, oil on panel, 90 x 72 cm (35 x 28 in) (Uffizi, Florence) 10 E; **115** *The Siege of Florence*, 1555-62, fresco (Leo X apartment, Palazzo Vecchio, Florence) 47 E

Verrocchio, byname of Andrea di Cione
116 *David*, before 1476, bronze, 126 cm (50 in) high (MNB) 25 E; **117** *Female head*, second half of 15th century, metal point, white and grey highlights on paper prepared with an orange ground, 26.7 x 22.5 cm (11 x 9 in) (Louvre, Paris) 8 E; **118** *Putto with a Dolphin*, c.1476, bronze, 67 cm (26 in) high (Palazzo Vecchio, Florence) 7 E

♦ INDEX

♦ CREDITS

The original and previously unpublished illustrations in this book may be reproduced only with the prior permission of Donati Giudici Associati, who hold the copyright. Abbreviations: t, top; b, bottom; c, centre; l, left; r, right.

ILLUSTRATIONS

Simone Boni, pp. 8-9, 11, 22-23, 28-29, 48-49, 50-51; L.R. Galante, pp. 16-17, 34-35, 36-37, 46-47, 56-57; Simone Boni – L.R. Galante, pp. 4-5; Simone Boni – Francesco Petracchi, pp. 54-55; Andrea Ricciardi, pp. 42-43; Sergio, pp. 6-7, 12-13.
COVER: Simone Boni
BACK COVER: Simone Boni
TITLE PAGE: L.R. Galante

WORKS OF ART REPRODUCED

Alinari, Florence: 29, 70, 77; Alinari/Giraudon: 18, 47, 67, 80, 90; Biblioteca Nazionale, Florence: 28; Bridgeman Art Library, London: 2, 24, 49, 75; British Library, London: 57; British Museum, London: 35; Casa Buonarroti, Florence: 63, 65, 72, 74, 78; DoGi: 3, 33, 101; DoGi/Serge Domingie, Marco Rabatti: 5, 12, 15, 16, 17, 19, 20, 22, 23, 25, 26, 27, 30, 31, 34, 36, 37, 40, 42, 43, 48, 50, 51, 54, 58, 59, 60, 61, 62, 66, 68, 69, 71, 73, 84, 85, 86, 89, 91, 95, 97, 98, 100, 108, 112, 113, 114, 115, 116, 118; DoGi/Mario Quattrone: 46, 52, 53, 55, 104; Serge Domingie, Marco Rabatti, Florence: 32, 39, 41, 81, 87, 92, 94, 96, 99, 103, 105, 107, 110, 111, 113; Graphische Sammlungen, Munich: 79; Eric Lessing, Vienna: 109; Museo di Palazzo Venezia, Rome: 106; Museo Nazionale, Naples: 6; National Gallery, London: 13, 93; Franco Cosimo Panini, Milan: 56; RMN:10, 38, 76, 82, 83, 88, 117; Scala, Florence: 4, 9, 11, 102; Vatican Museums, Rome: 1, 7, 8, 14, 64; Victoria and Albert Museum, London: 21.
Cover (clockwise): Alinari/Giraudon: q; DoGi/Serge Domingie, Marco Rabatti: a, c, e, f, g, h, j, k, l, n, o; DoGi/Mario Quattrone: u; Serge Domingie, Florence: s; RMN: i; Vatican Museums, Rome: b, d, m, r, t, v.
Back cover: DoGi/Serge Domingie, Marco Rabatti.
PHOTOGRAPHS

Achim Bednorz: p. 54b; DoGi: pp. 18c, 49, 57b; DoGi/Serge Domingie, Marco Rabatti: pp. 18tl, 18-19, 32, 42tr, 42cl, 43t; DoGi/Mario Quattrone: p. 18bl; Serge Domingie, Marco Rabatti, Florence: p. 42c; Liberto Perugi: 61tl.